SPARK

IGNITE INITIATIVE. WE'RE BETTER TOGETHER.

BRADLEY CHARBONNEAU

REPOSSIBLE

PRAISE FOR EVERY SINGLE DAY
A QUICK SELECTION OF BOOK REVIEWS FROM PEOPLE WHO ARE NOT MY MOM

If you're new to my ~~work~~ play, you might like to have a quick read of what other books of mine have done to help transform the lives of readers just like you.

I hope Spark transforms and transcends as much as "Every Single Day" did.

I especially like how "P.C." writes below "There's a **spark** within me that has been relit."

I get my inspiration and content from you and I hope to keep up that connection.

∽

"Somehow, I found myself devouring this today. It's rare that I allow myself this indulgence as the list of what I need to be doing in my head is endless.

Deliciousness to my soul, is the description that comes to mind as I reflect on my experience of consuming this book. I have no idea how to write a review and put into words **how deeply this resonated within me.**

There's a spark within me that has been relit. I know **ESD is the kindling I need to get the fire crackling and roaring** ... there are flames here that need to breathe and light the world.

Thank you Bradley Charbonneau for accepting the challenge of ESD, so that today, you could influence my ESD."

— 5 STARS FROM P.C. VIA AMAZON

∽

"I love how you handle **deep subjects in such a light-hearted way.**"

— Kay Bolden

~

"**Before reading this book I was ashamed of myself.**

For years I had called myself an artist but I knew the truth. I was only masquerading as one. ... But could I continue to call myself an artist when I stoped making artwork? The answers is no.

I am not entirely sure what happened to me from the time I was in college until now, eight years later. There was **a shift that took place** in my mind during that time.

I **developed a fear** of making artwork. I would always make excuses as to why I just couldn't create. I was too tired, the dog needed a bath, I needed to do dishes. What was the point of painting anyway **because no one would want to buy or look at my work** etc.

I have spent many years working dead end jobs just to pay bills. **I never even allowed myself a chance** at having a career because I would give up at the slightest failure or rejection.

The few times I did really try, I won awards at competitions.

I now have a two-year-old son. I have used him as an **excuse** to not make art for the past two years. **I feel guilty** that I put so much blame on my son. Taking care of him was just a convenient excuse that is easily believed by most people.

After reading this book, there is no going back. I have no choice.

I make artwork everyday and I am happy. ... I know there is no going back.

I was miserable with guilt and now I am not.

I was afraid to create and now I happy to learn once more.

When I started to draw again I was really rusty but I got through it. **I find time** even though I take care of my son all day and I babysit my nephew for eight and a half hours a day.

I wrote this review in the hope that I could inspire someone else to change their life.

Take the Every Single Day challenge. Read this book it just might change your life."

— Paige

"The author shows us how to get past "**analysis paralysis**" to actually start projects and see them through until completion.

A theme of this book is to **dream about doing something until the dream itself is internalized along with the willingness to progress toward goal completion in iterative steps taken each day.** Readers will learn the importance of getting past inertia in order to begin complex tasks and progress toward a completion date with certainty.

Everyone who moves toward a meritorious goal must first start, stumble, reassess and move ahead with a refined approach toward reaching the goals set forth at the outset. **Very few, if any, tasks are completed with zero failure points or stumbles.** A strong point of the book is that the author sets up readers for roadblocks which must be overcome as part of the learning process. The book could be labelled alternatively as "what it takes to succeed"!"

— Dr. Joseph S. Maresca, Amazon "Hall of Fame" Reviewer

"**Maybe you've let your dreams rust.**

Author Bradley Charbonneau has published several children's books and travel books, but in this 'self-help' genre he **unveils his own secrets for making life meaningful and successful.**

... the author opens the gates to his pathway for fulfillment and success. '**I transformed myself when I made the decision to change my behavior.**' He places bold statements throughout to make sure he has our attention, phrases such as '**Dreaming the dream was a whole lot easier than living the dream.**'

This fine book encourages us to take a very deep breath, start afresh, and make or lives what they CAN be. A very fine book."

— Grady Harp, Amazon "Hall of Fame" Top 100 Reviewer

∾

"This author has provided an excellent "how to" book, to **move past procrastination,** and **getting past fear**—teaching the reader how things made habitual can result in transformational success. This book could be **a really important read for the new, young person looking to "start" his life journey,** or switch directions after a rocky start. His writing is humorous, friendly, and engaging. I have bought two copies - one for both of my adult children."

— Robert Enzenauer

∾

" ... for anyone with **dreams hidden in the attic, cellar or heart.**"

— Amazon Reviewer

"He lights a path that you can choose to walk down."

— Ray Simon, accomplished speaker, and a no-longer-secret trumpet player

"A **very earnest sharing** by someone who has found his destiny and a way to achieve it."

— Bandaluse

Copyright © 2021 by Bradley Charbonneau

All rights reserved.

No part of this book may be reproduced in any form or by any electronic or mechanical means, including information storage and retrieval systems, without written permission from the author, except for the use of brief quotations in a book review.

❦ Created with Vellum

"With patience and persistence, even the smallest act of discipleship or the tiniest ember of belief can become a blazing bonfire of a consecrated life. In fact, that's how most bonfires begin - as a simple spark."

— Dieter F. Uchtdorf

DEDICATION
FOR LI & LU

Well, but also for Pepper.
Without Pepper, we never would have had one of those orange and blue bouncy balls and "The Secret of Kite Hill" might never have been discovered.

A Note about Li & Lu

My wife Saskia and I have two sons: Li & Lu. Those aren't their real names. I'm choosing to use their stage names in order to keep the flow of the story going.
But it's also to protect them from the paparazzi. With the probable future breakout success of the Li & Lu series, it's only fair to protect them as a father and potential tour manager should.
They are both available for interviews anytime. However, Wednesday evenings are basketball practice for Lu and Li needs to catch up on his math homework if he wants to achieve the levels of secret mathematical wisdom displayed in book five of the series, "Driehoek."
If you'd like to contact them directly, you can probably find them on Instagram although they rarely (OK fine, never) post about their literary

achievements and it's usually more along the lines of photos with fries and expensive sneakers.
This book is for them.

CONTENTS

Prologue   1
Foreword   3

PART I
WHY

1. Introduction: Embers   7
2. The quarter-inch drill bit, sparks, and expectations   9
3. Message in a Bottle   11
4. Let's create a family tradition   13
5. Rina   15

PART II
WHO

6. Introduction: Campers   19
7. The Widow and the Orphan   21
8. Gavin   24
9. LIFO: Last In, First Out   28
10. Maggie   30

PART III
WHAT

11. Introduction: Fire   37
12. It's an Experiment   40
13. The Great Unknown   42
14. Craig   44
15. Create more than you consume   47
16. Arlene   50

PART IV
WHEN

17. Introduction: Kindling   57
18. It's Now or Never   59
19. Rich   62

20. Lizz	64
21. Lorena	66

PART V
HOW

22. Introduction: Sparks	71
23. Replace Car Engine in Two Steps	73
24. Halfway will never finish	75
25. Create a Conflict	76
26. Meg	79
27. Want to truly learn something? Learn it through your kids.	81
28. How to make friends and influence...your kids	85
29. Brad	88
30. Don't talk about the project. Start the project.	90
31. Keep it legal, but keep it real	93
32. Linda	96

PART VI
CAMPFIRE STORIES

33. Introduction: Matches	101
34. How to instill creativity in your children in three not-so-easy steps.	104
35. Loss leaders, sales, flea markets and 12-year olds who want new shoes.	107
36. Make money, teach your kids math, and clean the house...at the same time.	112
37. How would your own kid sell his own book?	117

PART VII
GLOW

38. Spark Campfire	123
39. Questions for Parents	125
Afterword	127
Acknowledgments	129
Relationship	131
About the Author	133
Also by Bradley Charbonneau	135
The End	137

PROLOGUE

In March of 2014, I wrote "The Secret of Kite Hill" together with my two sons (then 8 and 10 years old).

It was both "just a fun little thing we did" and a "monumental shift in who I was" at the time.

This is precisely my point, my philosophy, and my drive.

As cheesy as the cliché is, that little book changed my life.

A silly little 38-page story about walking home from school with the dog.

But it wasn't the book itself that did it.

It was the process.

It was reading chapters aloud as they lay nestled in their beds—even on a school night.

It was Lu asking, after I had finished reading a chapter, "Then what happened?" only to have me respond that I didn't know because it was *his* story and what happened would have to be created in his own imagination.

It was getting them to sit down and record the audiobook version (no chips here).

It was bribing them with tortilla chips for non-audio-recording sessions.

It was whining and pleading, "No, dad. Not the book project again!"

It was Li building a book trailer on our brand-new iPad.

It was determination.

It was creating something from nothing.

It was afterwards when my too-cool-for-school older son said to his buddies (and didn't know I was within earshot), "Yeah, I have a book on Amazon."

It was the "Side Effects" of the action taken.

It was the "Hidden and Unknown Benefits" of co-creating.

It was starting, muddling through, persevering, and getting something finished. We got it *done*.

Together with two young boys.

This is my story.

This is their story.

This is the stories of others who have traveled a similar path.

My hope with this book is that it becomes your story.

Welcome to Spark.

FOREWORD
BY GAVIN REESE

"The world always seems brighter when you've just made something that wasn't there before."

— Neil Gaiman

This is an important book, maybe the most important you'll read this year. I don't believe I could possibly overstate the significance of what Bradley's shared with the rest of us, but I'll leave it to you to decide. For me, this is most important concept in nearly a decade.

Spark is about relationships, connections, and quality time spent with the most important people in your life. Whether you're considering putting this to work with your kids, grandkids, nieces, or nephews, we're all searching for ways to capture the moments of their growth, encapsulate them, and ensure we keep a piece of time that never gets to grow up. The process Bradley explains in Spark does just that. The most beautiful aspect of this is that you aren't required to be an author, writer, or wordsmith to make this work for you and yours. It helps, but it isn't necessary. The end product is not the mark of success here. It is only the journey getting there that matters at all.

I struggled to find ways to engage with the kids in our family for years. How do I get them to put down the tablet, turn off the TV, engage in an actual dialogue, and spend quality time with us before they grow up and these opportunities are lost forever? They all quickly grew tired of me asking what they'd learned each day in school, and I had grown equally tired of the one-word responses to my investigation of their lives. How it is that all the kids I know never learn anything in school each day?

I can't say that all those obstacles forever changed after I met Bradley and put his co-author process to work, but I can tell you that our family has a new hobby. Together. Everyone's engaged, willing, and eager, even if they're a little too cool to openly show it all the time.

I grew up in a divorced family, and I've always wanted to have that romanticized experience with my dad in which we rebuilt a car together. Beyond the refurbished hot rod, we'd have this block of time, a few months spent together over a few years, that can't be lost no matter what happens to the car. Spark can help you and your treasured littles have that same experience. Hours, days even, spread over weeks and months creating something together that everyone's excited about and happy to be a part of. You won't have a 1957 Chevy Bel Air two-door post at the end, but you will have a book. A document that forever records what your little's life was like at that moment in time. Repeat this every year or so, and you'll have a catalogue history of their growth and development. More importantly, you'll have the memories of doing this together. Those moments can never be taken away, regardless of what life and the world have in store for all of you.

See? I told you this book was important. It has been for me and it can be for you.

-- Gavin Reese, author of multiple thriller series and co-author of Space Dogs with his niece, Maddi Lager.

PART I
WHY

"Because your imagination can change the world."

— Neil Gaiman

1

INTRODUCTION: EMBERS

"At times our own light goes out and is rekindled by a spark from another person. Each of us has cause to think with deep gratitude of those who have lighted the flame within us."

— Albert Schweitzer

Although this book is supposedly about kids and for kids, I'm going to let you in on a little secret early on. Yes, I realize we're in the introduction of part one of the book, but hear me out. I'll be brief.

We, dear parents, dear adults, are the ones who probably need the spark.

Yep, this entire book started out with the intention of rekindling that spark within our children. But you know what? They are like, if you'll excuse my tireless visuals of fire and kindling and embers, that perfectly constructed bonfire with the pine needles and thin strips of bark gathered so carefully. It's all ready to go. There's just enough air and fuel and all it needs is a little spark.

Meanwhile, we adults are more like that smoldering pile of wet charcoal the night after the bonfire. Then it rained.

As I've worked on this book, interviewed moms and uncles, bakers and musicians, authors and artists, I've learned that although the kids might need that one little spark to get the fire started, we are the ones who are going to bask in the warm glow of the adventure, this experiment, this time in our lives.

Meanwhile, once that fire has caught, they're looking for marshmallows and a stick to roast them on.

They have the energy, the creativity, and the bottomless imaginations. We're here to provide that initial spark to get this campfire started.

We're after the lasting, glowing, and warm embers that will endure far beyond this one scene in the long play of our lives--and the many acts to come for our kids.

Embers. Warm. Glowing. Alive.

That's why we're doing this.

2

THE QUARTER-INCH DRILL BIT, SPARKS, AND EXPECTATIONS

NO, REALLY, WHAT ARE WE AFTER HERE?

"No one buys a quarter-inch drill bit because they need a quarter-inch drill bit. What they need is a quarter-inch hole."

— TED LEVITT

In an interview with Tim Ferris on his podcast, Seth Godin explains Ted Levitt's quarter-inch drill bit theory.

"What you need is a place to put the books that are cluttering your bedroom. But you don't even really need that. What you need is the way you will feel when your spouse thanks you for cleaning things up. What you really need are safety and security and a feeling that you did something that was important."

— SETH GODIN

What are we after here, anyway?

As Seth Godin says over and over, "No one wants to buy a quarter-inch drill bit." People don't lay awake at night dreaming about it.

They don't talk to their friends about it. They don't really care about the drill bit.

What do they want?

In his example: praise from his wife. A feeling of pride. Safety and security.

In a book about writing a book with your kids, I really shouldn't say this, but... it's not about the book. It's about with the kids.

Then there's that last bit from Seth Godin, "a feeling that you did something that was important."

There you have it. The big secret of this book: a feeling that you did something that was important.

When it comes down to it, that's what I'm after.

If you'd like to know what I'm after, it's even easier. It's the same thing. For me, it's a feeling that something I did was important if I can help you feel like something you did was important.

That's it.

The rest is details and process and deciding and willpower and scheduling and deciding to make this happen. Deciding that you're going to be one of those people who do things like this.

What are things like this?

Something we feel is important.

∼

Flashback

On the actual Kite Hill itself, San Francisco, California

> "Who's going to buy a book about our stupid story on Kite Hill anyway?" asked Lu. He had a point.
> What I couldn't quite eloquently (or effectively) explain to my then 8-year-old son was that the book wasn't what I was after. What I was after was the experience of working on the book together with him and his brother.

3

MESSAGE IN A BOTTLE

IF DREAMS ARE TRAPPED INSIDE AND AREN'T LET OUT, ARE THEY STILL REAL?

"It's the possibility of having a dream come true that makes life interesting."

— PAULO COELHO

When dreams come true I imagine fireworks and tears of joy and some kid with a huge grin on her face. This, of course, is after the dream was created, given permission to exist, and realized.

But what about those dreams that are still bottled up inside of a child (or worse: an adult) that were never given permission to come out and play?

Frankly, I wonder what's worse: to have started a dream and never quite achieved it? Or to have never let the genie out of the bottle to see what happens?

They both sound pretty awful to me.

Which is why I want to set them free. Make sure we pull them out of our kids even when we might think they're stuck.

You know that nasty hair in the shower drain? You think you just have a little bit of it and you pull it up but then you get this big, nasty glob of hair?

The dreams of your child might be like that. Hiding out in the drain of the shower needing just the tiniest of extra efforts and patience to set it free.

Is it time to check the shower drain?

Is it time to check what dreams might be stuck in your child?

Is it time to check what dreams might be stuck in you?

4

LET'S CREATE A FAMILY TRADITION
PICK A BOOK, ANY BOOK. READ PAGE ONE.

"It's true, Christmas can feel like a lot of work, particularly for mothers. But when you look back on all the Christmases in your life, you'll find you've created family traditions and lasting memories. Those memories, good and bad, are really what help to keep a family together over the long haul."

— Caroline Kennedy

That was it. Nothing earth shattering. Just trying to make every night a little special, just add a little spice, just a little something to remind us that we're alive, that each day, that each night of our lives is a little different if we choose to make it so.

No, it didn't turn into an annual tradition. In fact, we never did it again. But this book isn't so much about me and my family and what worked and what didn't. It's about sprinkling ideas into you and your family and seeing what sticks, what works, what flops, and just giving it a shot.

It's mostly about giving it a shot.

Flashback

Haunted house of books. Santa Barbara, California
We're staying in a friend of a friend's house that must have thousands of books. They're everywhere. It's an old house with more character than Meryl Streep. We're only spending one night, but I think I could spend a year. It's going to be hard to leave tomorrow.
We got home late and it's just the boys and I and I didn't want to go right to sleep.
How do you begin traditions? Something that you do with your family every year. Who thinks it up? Who keeps it going? Just start. See what happens.
Before I lost their attention, there were just so many books. What could we do with them? There was a front room with cozy chairs and something of a loveseat. The whole place was a throwback at least 50 years. All as if it hadn't been touched in 50 years.
"OK, let's all read page one of whatever book you pick up. Just read it to yourself. Then we can tell each other what it was about. OK?"
I was surprised, but they went for it.
Li got "To Kill a Mockingbird." Lu got something about London streets and I got "For Whom the Bell Tolls."
We all read in silence for a few minutes and then explained what we had read.

5

RINA

A MEAN CORNBREAD AND THE ONE RECIPE COOKBOOK

"I think in terms of chapters. Every time I finish a movie, it's a chapter. When one of my kids graduates from school, that's a chapter."

— STEVEN SPIELBERG

Rina is something of a perfectionist. She's an excellent photographer, but will wait for just the right light, or until the child turns slightly and then she's got it.

Everything she does has style to it. It's beautiful, inspiring, and complete.

While we were brainstorming about "Spark" experiments for her and her children, she brought up the idea of a cookbook.

"My boys can make a mean cornbread," Rina said with pride.

We talked more and I could see her dreaming up the photography for the book, the perfect font to use for each recipe heading. She'd probably dig up old family recipes and add a splash of the nature of her children to combine the old with the new.

"How many recipes do you need for a cookbook?" she asked as we walked in the forest.

In a rare flash of brilliance and mathematical wizardry, I calculated how long it was going to take her to do the photo shoots, lay out the pages properly, get her kids to look just right while stirring the cornbread dough, multiplied all of that by the number of family recipes to be added in and then calculated time for editing and retouching of photos and I had her answer.

"One," I said as someone with far more experience in cookbook publishing than I have and a generous helping of one of my larger goals: Get It Done.

Her jaw fell, her eyes widened, and her shoulders dropped as the pressure was removed from the scene.

Instead of loading her up with a lengthy project, hardbound cover production, and a heaping spoonful of responsibility, I gave her permission.

Permission to play.

To make this fun. To Get This Done. Done is Won.

One chapter. One recipe. One photo for all I care. Here, Rina, we'll even give you some title options:

1. Two Boys and their Dough
2. Cornbread Like You've Never Tasted
3. The One Recipe Cookbook: Cornbread
4. Kids' Kornbread Kookbook
5. Cornbread for Kids

We're still in the Why section of this book. I'll probably hammer you over the head with this, but I want us to FINISH a project.

I don't want Rina to make the perfect cookbook with 43 recipes from 8 generations on 256 glossy pages that will show up on my doorstep in the year 2037.

We're building a time capsule and you don't keep adding to those. You do it, bury it, and move on.

The one-recipe cookbook will be in stores as soon as...uh, Rina?

PART II
WHO

"I have no special talent. I am only passionately curious."

— Albert Einstein

INTRODUCTION: CAMPERS

"Fires can't be made with dead embers, nor can enthusiasm be stirred by spiritless men. Enthusiasm in our daily work lightens effort and turns even labor into pleasant tasks."

— James Baldwin

Let's do a little roll call:

1. **You?** Here! (reading these words)
2. **Me?** Check. (writing these words)
3. **Them?** Present! (probably not right here, right now, but they're around somewhere)

Oh good, we're all here.

1. **You:** parent, aunt, grandfather, adult of some kind.
2. **Me:** parent, uncle, occasional adult, author of this book and five other books I wrote together with my kids.
3. **Them:** kids. They don't even need to be yours. If you don't

have a daughter or son, a niece or nephew or Samantha down the street all work just fine.

I already don't like the "us" versus "them" I seemingly have going on in my numbered list above. My goal is to transform all of us into a communal "we."

This section is called "Who" and I just wanted to make sure we're checked in at the same campground. You might think that I'll stop at some point with the whole "spark" and "ember" and "campfire" mentions. But I won't.

7

THE WIDOW AND THE ORPHAN
EVEN JUST THE TITLE OF THIS CHAPTER MAKES ME WANT TO WRITE A STORY.

"The way to connect to people is to relate to who they are and do something that stretches you outside of your comfort zone."

— Stacy Brown-Philpot

For most of this book, I'll talk about "you" and "them" in terms that we usually understand to be:

1. Parent
2. Child

But it could very easily be:

1. Uncle and niece,
2. Single guy and neighbor kid,
3. or how about widow and orphan?

I have a specific person in mind with this concept. She's 94 years old and is sharp as a tack. She has stories to tell until the cows come home (and long after they've gone to sleep). She has more energy than most people a quarter of her age and I've only ever heard the following request in the presence of her:

"Could you slow down grandma? We can't keep up."

She's a machine.

Here's a wild thought for Spark: what if we could connect widows and orphans? Widowers and the girl down the street who doesn't really connect with her parents?

I'm not talking about adoption. I'm talking about a 1-month, start-to-finish, short book they'd create together.

What if Spark brought together two strangers who then collaborated on something? Who knows, maybe the chemistry didn't quite gel and it fizzled out after a week.

But what if something happened?

They met a few times and started to talk. The little girl wanted to tell a story about her doll and her dog and how they talk to each other but nobody ever wanted to listen.

What if the old man in the senior living community listened intently to the girl and whispered to her, "I can hear them talking now, Nina, but I can't quite understand what they're saying. Could you translate for me?"

Can you see the story sparkling to life in front of the girl's eyes? Her imagination would explode and she would have a captive audience who truly wanted to hear her story and what the doll was saying to the dog.

In 30 days, they'd have a finished book. Things got a little out of hand and the old man eventually called in the nurse to transcribe everything the girl was saying in the story as his hands got tired from all that writing. The three of them sat around the lunch table and "The Adventures of Fifi and Fido" came to life.

Grandpa and the nurse thought things were all good and done until the next time the little girl came by and said, "I have another story. Could you help me again?"

I see Sparks flying, embers warming, and moving in closer to the campfire to get going on book number two in the "Fifi & Fido" series.

Do you know anyone in a senior living community who might like to connect? How about a child who could use an ear to listen?

Maybe we could make this work. Let me know if you have any ideas at spark.repossible.com.

8

GAVIN

DON'T HAVE SON OR DAUGHTER OF YOUR OWN? NOT A PROBLEM.

"The hidden child wants to be able to participate and to co-create in art, rather than being simply an admiring viewer."

— CHRISTIAN MORGENSTERN

What I love about Gavin's story is that he doesn't have a son or daughter--but he has a niece. I mention this because it opened up (like Grand Canyon-size open) my dreams about where the Spark project could go and immediately addresses comments I've had from adults without kids who say, "But I don't have kids." Also, see the chapter titled, "The Widow and The Orphan."

Here's how Gavin began:

My then-seven-year-old niece, Maddi, loves books, and she'd shown some interest in my burgeoning writing career and occasionally asked questions about it.

"She'd show some interest" is the key phrase here. Pounce on any interest kids show (or try to hide!) and run with it.

Here's more directly from Gavin:

Maddi freely offered her opinions and wants, so I guided the dialogue and our objectives to ensure the story had a simple plot, some tension, and positive resolution. We also needed a catchy, unusual title, which she provided: Space Dogs. Within a few minutes, we created a project in which she was intellectually interested and emotionally invested.

I'm going to highlight again: "intellectually interested and emotionally invested."

I'd venture to say that we only need one of those two:

1. Intellectually interested
2. Emotionally invested

If you can get both, you're pretty much set. But if I had to pick one, I think "emotionally invested" might get you further. Let's add a body part to Gavin's list:

1. Intellectually interested (brain)
2. Emotionally invested (heart)

This entire operation, in my humble opinion, is an adventure of and for the heart. Yep, we'll learn some things and probably become a better writer or negotiator or story teller or illustrator along the way but what I'm after is the heart.

Back to Gavin:

Dostoevsky, it ain't. It's not supposed to be. It's a very simple and short story, but it fulfilled every objective I had at the outset of this project. Maddi contributed to a dialogue, an intellectual back-and-forth that required compromise and consideration of someone else's wants, thoughts, and opinions.

- Objectives? Check.
- Dialogue? Got it.
- Intellectual back-and-forth? Yep.

But then comes The Good Part. Gavin explains:

For me, this is very closely akin to the 1957 Bel Air two-door post that my dad and I haven't ever rebuilt together. It's an incredibly important, emotional anchor in our relationship. No matter what happens over the rest of our lifetimes, we'll have these moments we got to spend together. Nothing can take that away from us.

Can I do another bullet list?

- Emotional anchor? Check.
- Moments we got to spend together? Yep.
- Nothing can take that away from us. Got it.

I'm thrilled Maddi had some "intellectual back-and-forth." I'm not even sure how often I have "intellectual back-and-forth."

But the tear-in-my-eye-inducing "Nothing can take that away from us." is the experience of it, the co-creating they did, the dare-I-say "project completion" of working on something together, pulling through, and getting it done. Together.

I'm going to give you just a bit more of Gavin and drop in a teaser from their book:

The plot revolved around our extended family's collection of dogs. All but a few are lovable mutts, but a couple real-life scalawags among them had created tension that helped us craft the story. Two of our heroes had trouble getting along with another species; their differences were just too great to be friends. They decided to travel to space to seek out wisdom from other dogs that had found ways to befriend different creatures. They quickly acquired this new knowledge, returned home to Earth, and told everyone what they'd learned. All dogs live happily ever after.

All dogs live happily ever after? I think Maddi is onto something. Stay tuned for the sequel...

9

LIFO: LAST IN, FIRST OUT
YOU CAN'T FINISH IF YOU DON'T START.

"Finish last in your league and they call you idiot. Finish last in medical school and they call you doctor."

— Abe Lemons

Yeah, sorry for the "Last In, First Out" reference. It's from a production line in a factory. You see, I went to business school. Got a master's degree even. I feel like I have to throw around my knowledge sometimes to remind myself why I had to drudge through accounting for two years. I also need to grant myself the key to take off my necktie, to not take life so seriously, to get into the dirt with the kids, to think like they think, to let go of adult complexities, forget the degrees on the wall, and give myself permission to play. That's who we are allowed to be--or become.

Back to LIFO...

Think of a parking lot. Did you ever go to a game where it was so poorly organized that people just parked behind each other and if you got there last, you were going to have to get out first? That's Last In, First Out.

First In, First Out could be that same ballgame parking lot but then they open the (front) gates so those who got there first need to leave first. Another typical First In, First Out is a factory assembly line.

So the product (or in this case, your project) might be Last In, but there's a chance it's First Out. In other words, you might be a little late getting started, but **the fact that you're starting increases your chance of finishing.**

How much?

I'm going to call it a 100% increase. How do I know? It's easy math. If you don't start, your chances of finishing are 0%. If you start, your chances increase from 0 to 1. Although, mathematically, just starting doesn't mean you'll finish. But not starting does equate to not being able to finish.

Where in the world am I going with this chapter? (That's a rhetorical question that I better answer in the next paragraph or I'm in trouble.)

If you're last in, you might truly be first out. Maybe you've procrastinated and hemmed and hawed and now have a better idea of what you're going to do and finally, somehow, from somewhere, maybe even from reading this chapter, you know you're going to do it.

You now have motivation, momentum, and you're more in a hurry than you were before.

You're not late to the party if the party is still going. You arrived.

Now your party can start.

∼

Flashback
Antelope Canyon, Motel Parking Lot, Page, Arizona
I have a pang of pain that I started all of this too late. My kids are getting older. I'm getting older. Maybe I missed the window of opportunity. I try not to worry about things I don't have control of. I also try not to regret what I cannot change. I'm reminded to keep going, to keep playing the game.

10

MAGGIE

HANDS UP: WHO HAS A LIFE GOAL TO WRITE A NOVEL BEFORE YOU'RE 50?

"A dream you dream alone is only a dream. A dream you dream together is reality."

— YOKO ONO

We're still in the section called Who. Although many (most?) of us might think this is all for the kids, we adults are not only active participants in the experiment, but we may well be the accidental subject.

Maggie writes for a living. In fact, many professionals write for a living: attorneys write up cases, doctors write reports, and managers write business plans. She's a professor at a university and her writing is nonfiction.

But Maggie wanted to write fiction. She also wanted to do it before she was 50.

- Enter stage left: Josh (son).
- Enter stage right: Matt (husband).

Now I don't know if Maggie's dream was to sit on her porch, sip iced tea, gaze out onto the lake, spend 14 years, and write the Great American Novel.

When you dare to co-create and make the project a team effort, flexibility is key.

Her husband Matt relates how it played out:

"It dawned on us that Maggie is a prolific writer in her profession (at a university). I'm an engineer at an aerospace company that understands physics."

Now the part where Maggie and Matt's story takes a turn down the creative path is what he says next. Because from the view on the sidelines, I'm pretty sure no one is yet seeing a clear path towards writing a book together.

"We thought we could teach physics to children along with telling a really fun story. Maggie's got all the writing skills, I've got all the physics."

This is clearly a family after my own mathematics-loving heart. Only a select few would have "teach physics" and "children" and "fun story" in the same sentence. It was obvious we were going to get along.

Then their son Josh comes into the picture.

"Josh can tell us what references work for a 8-12 year old kids. What's funny, what isn't funny. What references are good, what references are way too old."

"We really have the three people we need to write a successful book."

They took their diverse backgrounds and calculated that they had what they needed.

I feel a little math coming on:

1. A university professor
2. An aerospace engineer
3. An 11-year-old boy

That's doesn't scream, "I know! They should write a book together!" It doesn't add up.

But can you follow me here with where this is going?

It does add up.

It adds up perfectly.

1 + 1 + 1 = 3

Then we get into exponential mathematics--and things get really good.

Maggie is fulfilling her dream of writing fiction before she's 50.

Matt said the book project improved his marriage and he got to write some science fiction to boot.

Josh is thrilled to be their sounding board and "editorial consultant."

1 + 1 + 1 > 3

Maggie + Matt + Josh > 3

It adds up to more than the sum of the parts. Each one could have done something on their own but because they did it together it increased the sum exponentially.

The more Matt and Maggie and I talked, the more Side Effects the book project had--on all of them.

Here are a few highlights from our conversation.

"They want it to be funny."

— JOSH (LETTING HIS PARENTS KNOW WHAT ELEMENTARY-AGED KIDS WANT TO READ)

"It really brought us closer together and continues to bring us closer together as a family."

— MAGGIE

"The vast majority of the work we did on the book was on super long drives to my mom's house. We would just bring 10 or 12 chapters of the book and read them aloud. Josh would comment on it. 12 hours go by pretty quick. Our son stays engaged for 12 hours."

— Matt

"An 11-year-old boy getting to tell his 48-year-old dad how it is."

— Matt

If you'd like to read more about their adventures in fiction, come on over to spark.repossible.com and see how they mix baseball, physics, and "Strxia, a parallel world facing certain ruin."

PART III
WHAT

"If we knew what it was we were doing, it would not be called research, would it?"

— Albert Einstein

INTRODUCTION: FIRE

"In everyone's life, at some time, our inner fire goes out. It is then burst into flame by an encounter with another human being. We should all be thankful for those people who rekindle the inner spirit."

— Albert Schweitzer

You'd think the "What" section of this book would be simple. Here goes one option:
What are we creating here:

1. A book
2. A workshop
3. A short story
4. A cookbook
5. A song

Etc.

Although I don't disagree with the above list, it's not what I'm after. Yes, those are the "things" we're making, but I'm going to go cliché and use, "It's the journey, not the destination."

Here's a list that's a little harder to, well, hold in your hand:

1. Experience
2. Creating (better: co-creating)
3. Experiment
4. Memories
5. Time capsule
6. Love

I'm going to go out on a limb and create a quote that sums it up for me:

"Love is the overlap of the experience of two people."

- Person one can have an experience.
- Person two can have an experience.

But when person one and person two have that experience together, it's different.

- Yellow on its own is yellow.
- Green on its own is green.

But the overlap, the Venn diagram of those two elements interacting with each other becomes something different: blue.

Person one didn't have blue. Person two didn't have blue. But together, they made blue.

Yes, we'll write a book or compose a song. Great. But what I'm after is the experience of creating it together. It's not the same as two people creating separately. Yellow would still be yellow and green still green. Only together can they create blue.

Maybe it's a stretch, but what I see as the outcome or the result or benefit or side effect of Spark is, quite simply, love.

Love from one person needs love from another person to create love for each other.

I'm not talking about "I love you" and "I care about that person."

This is experience together. Working together towards a goal, finishing that goal, relishing in the success (and failures!) of the process.

Call me crazy, but that's what I call love.

You can still call me crazy.

But I have the recipe for love.

12

IT'S AN EXPERIMENT
WE CAN'T FAIL

"We often say that the biggest job we have is to teach a newly hired employee to fail intelligently... to experiment over and over again and to keep on trying and failing until he learns what will work."

— CHARLES KETTERING

If we were to call this thing we're doing with the kids a test, then we'd have two probable outcomes:

- Success
- Failure

Which is why we're not going to call it a test. Or a project. Experiment.

Author's Note: I usually regret writing "Author's Note" as I'm often trying to explain something or more often making some excuse for why something isn't the way it was maybe going to be. But for the longest time, I was calling these things we're doing with our kids "projects."

What happened was that it quickly went to the dreaded *Science*

Project at school that no one wanted to do: not the parent, not the child, not even really so much the science teacher.

Except for those projects that were unexpected or unknown. They maybe didn't follow the guidelines quite right. Or they forgot to read the instructions at all. It turned from a project to an experiment.

13

THE GREAT UNKNOWN

EXPERIMENT: NOUN: AN ACT OR OPERATION FOR THE PURPOSE OF DISCOVERING SOMETHING UNKNOWN

"Experiments rarely turn out the way they're supposed to. That's why they're called experiments."

— Dawson Church

Here's how things might go:
1. You read this book,
2. You write a short book together with your 9-year-old daughter,
3. She discovers she has a talent for drawing maps and something of a sixth sense for history,
4. The UN happens to stumble upon your book (about maps and dragonflies),
5. They hire her (you, dear parent, get to tag along) to come to the former Yugoslavia to redraw the borders that will reallocate the land among Croatia and Slovenia,
6. She has a job waiting for her when she turns 16 at the UN

and until then is named honorary cartographer extraordinaire.

It could happen. But this could also happen.

1. You read this book,
2. You write a short book together with your 8-year-old son,
3. It turns out, as much as I'm a fan of tortilla chips, he absolutely can't stand tortilla chips,
4. This goes so far as to stop the entire book adventure and instead you create a recipe for corn-free tortilla chips that taste just how he likes them (you're looking into a patent),
5. You write it out and take a photo of the new chip,
6. Uncle Ray at Thanksgiving said the newly-invented chip was, "Pretty good."
7. Your son is proud.
8. You are proud that your son is proud.
9. Nothing more is ever said about it again.
10. Until he's 32.

That might happen, too.

That's just it. I have no idea what's going to happen. But here's what's going to happen with inaction.

1. You don't do anything.
2. Nothing happens.

That's another option.

This is the usual option. 4 out of 5 dentists usually recommend this option. I'm trying not to say that one is better than another. They're just different.

It's an experiment. We don't know the outcome.

That's usually a good thing.

4 out of 5 times.

14

CRAIG
IT WAS KIND OF ON A WHIM.

"Where words fail, music speaks."

— Hans Christian Andersen

I'm transcribing here snippets from Craig because I can't describe his story any better than he did. Here he is:

"I'm big into meditation and I'm big into raising kids consciously and I thought, 'One day I'm going to sit down and write a simple kids' meditation.'"

"I sat down and wrote and I'm not really a writer but you can tell when something is flowing and it did. 20 minutes later I had this little script and I ran it by Emily and I ran it by my wife. There was very little editing. As a test, I thought I would have Emily just record the narration so I turned the microphone on and she recorded it and it seemed fitting."

"It was one of those projects that came together very very quickly. It still needs a little refining maybe, but that's the beauty of it, it was quick and easy and simple."

I need to stop Craig right there.

In one sentence, in fact, in 5 words, he put together 3 words that are rarely seen in the wild in the same savannah on a safari of creative projects with kids:

1. Quick
2. Easy
3. Simple

Sure, fine, 1 of the 3 we see all the time. Maybe 2 of the 3 we have together on a good day. But all three? This is like the lion and the elephant and the rhinoceros are all hanging out at the watering hole long enough for you to adjust the zoom on your brand-new camera you bought for safari.

In other words, it just doesn't happen.

But then with Craig and his daughter Emily, that's exactly what happened.

I add Craig's story here because I'd like to document, for the record, that those 3 words can be possible, that they can happen at the same time with a project with your kids. In case you're still on the floor reeling from those 3 words together about a project with your kids, I'll put them here again:

1. Quick
2. Easy
3. Simple

In case you're wondering what might come to mind when I think about creating "The Secret of Kite Hill," there are, ahem, other descriptive terms that might come up. Oh, I don't know:

1. Torture by literature
2. Bribery with salty potato products
3. Imagination chaos on a school night

No, really. Those were off the top of my head. We need to get back to Craig and Emily.

"Encouraged her to be a part of the creative process, to do some editing, to share some opinions, and I think that helped. It wasn't me telling her what to do every step of the way. I treated her like an equal co-creator in the process and she was."

Emily was a co-creator in the process. Her dad asked for and valued her opinions. She was an integral part of it all.

"I just asked for help, asked for her insights."

"It's confidence building and shows that you have respect for their opinions and insights."

"I haven't had a lot of people listen to it yet."

I've listened to the meditation called "The Wishing Well" and it's beautiful. For more about Craig, Emily, and their music, come on over to the savannah at spark.repossible.com.

15

CREATE MORE THAN YOU CONSUME
MOST PEOPLE ARE PASSIVE. THEY TAKE INFORMATION IN.

> "One of the characteristics common to best-selling authors is a focus on creation. They are much more interested in producing information than consuming it."
>
> — Dawson Church

Have you ever noticed there aren't too many books for children on how to ride a bike?

While travel books can "make it almost like you're really there," you're not really there.

How about a study course for babies on how to walk? Complete with diagrams, charts, and a table that parents can fill in with progress.

TIP: babies can't read.

BONUS TIP: babies don't need a book to teach them how to walk, they just need to try, fall down, learn, and try again.

The book you're holding in your hands is my 14th book. Let's do a little math. What is 14 minus 14? Zero! Excellent. Book number one took me 36 years to write. Book number two took another 10 years.

When people ask me how I come up with the ideas on what to write about then I know they're not creators. I have too many ideas. I have so many words. I have descriptions and scenes and philosophies and topics I don't know much about but can't wait to learn about so I read and watch and then to really learn: I write.

To use the quote above and apply it to myself:

I am much more interested in producing information than consuming it.

This part is where the physics gets a little difficult to explain, but by creating, I am actually "getting" more than I am "giving."

By doing, I am learning more than reading or watching or listening to someone telling me to do.

Yet, here we are, here I am going on and on about doing and creating and writing and you're reading.

I can't write your book for you. I can't paint your painting or create your recipe or compose your song. Well, yes, of course I could, but that's not the point. The point is for you to do, to make, to build, to write, to create.

Because let's face the cold, hard facts: there is no substitute.

- Through creating, I am learning.
- By creating, I am giving.
- By creating, I am receiving more than I am giving.

I'm not suggesting we all become prolific creators who…OK, fine, that's exactly what I'm suggesting.

If there are "secrets" in this book that I wish to convey only to those who read it through and through, this is one of them: create.

- Consuming is passive
- Creating is active

If you read this book and think about creating an experiment with your kid it's like reading the manual on riding a bike. There is no substitute for experience.

Most people are passive. They take information in.

We can't change the past. We can create our present reality. By creating our present, we are setting the trajectory of our future.

Yes, I have a book planned called: Create.

Because it's just that important.

16

ARLENE
THAT MEAN GIRL THING

"When you're nice, you're not bullying people. But when you're kind, you stand up against the bully."

— Daniel Lubetzky

"*...*A journey of self discovery using NLP, Hypnotherapy, Magic, and Meditation." Do you ever have it where your kid's school has a program or an event but it sounds so good you'd like to do it yourself? I had this with one of the high schools we looked at for my son because it had a sport program that included surfing for a week in Spain. Then I had it with what Arlene did together with her daughters.

"I didn't want to just talk to them anymore, it wasn't making a difference. I wanted to model it for them, teach the girls tools they could use. Really and truly, my intention was for them to come to know that they were powerful and indeed magic."

Arlene's two young girls (7 and 9) were being bullied at school-- even by friends.

"I wanted to create something with the girls using the stories they told me to help to empower them."

She tried to get girls together to work through a program. At her first attempt to get girls' parents on board, they all said no.

She looked further. Found other girls, other parents. With the new group of girls, she asked them what they wanted from the workshop.

- Gained Confidence
- Finding their voice
- Healthy Relationships and Positive Lifestyle
- Support for the development of leadership and life skills
- Sense of belonging or connected
- Increased Community Connections
- Encourage the awareness of their core values, personal interests, strengths and attributes, and above all, knowing that they were magic.

Who wouldn't want all that? Now the parents were on board when they saw the list.

To this point, I remind us all to know our own goals of our experiment. My own simple goal back in 2014 was to write a book in a month and get it on Amazon. Simple goal, deadline, done.

Arlene has loftier yet still very accomplish-able goals and that helped get the parents to believe in what she was doing--and it helps us and the kids, too.

"Building the program was easy, having them participate in the program was my challenge. It was easy to get the buy in from the parents. I simply gave them the list up above, but getting the buy in from the girls proved to be difficult at times."

Sure, the list above was great to convince that parents that this whole endeavor was a good idea. But how to get the kids involved?

"We worked together from week to week, and at points and time, one would project onto the other, or onto themselves. There were times when I had to leave one child for alone time, to simply feel what they were feeling and held the space for what came up. What I discovered while running this program was that they absolutely loved the magic.

Each week I would incorporate a nature walk. We would feel the trees and the different energy of the trees, and then I would would have them tune into each other, to feel how each person had a unique signature. One week we played in a field, I had one girl on her own at the end of one field, facing away from the group. She would keep her eyes closed, building upon the energy work we had taught in prior weeks, I had the girls ground their energy and create a bubble of their energy around them. Then one by one a child would step forward towards the girl facing the other direction. The girl with her back turned was instructed to come name who was coming towards her as soon as she felt them.

The results were amazing. 3 of the 5 girls were 100%, while I could see the two girls who guessed incorrectly, second guessed their intuition just before saying the name. As awesome as this was, it created a sense of comparison between them all. And though my intention was to empower, the two girls closed themselves off for the rest of the class."

What I'm proposing in Spark is an experiment. An experiment means we're testing, trying, playing. It's not perfect yet and maybe never needs to be. What works we can do more of. What doesn't work we can do less of.

Arlene continued learning, revamping, and playing.

"There were great learnings in this program that I would incorporate into others, it was a 2 steps forward, 1 step back full of insights about how they saw themselves.

My own daughter sat out some of the time, and no matter what I did, she would not join the group. I simply had to work with what I had.

Would I do this again? Absolutely!

In following up with the girls, they've all forgotten their tools... so one key next step is, how do I maintain and empower the girls so that they are inspired to continue using them? I ran this program 2 years ago and when I see most of the girls, they'd love for me to run it again. One child can't seem to look me in the eyes, such a curious thing and regardless, I just might run the program this summer, make it bigger and better.

There's nothing like being reminded of the magic within.

Empowered with tools and skills, reminded of your uniqueness and playing outside under the sun."

Magic? Outdoors? Empowerment? What could go wrong? What could go right?

When I first started this project, I had two quick ideas:

1. Bradley writes book with kids and shares experiences and instructions on how others can do it too.
2. Bradley's story is OK. We need other stories that are not about 2 boys and a book.

What I like about Arlene's story is that I never would have thought of it. That's what makes it different and new and exciting.

If you'd like to hear more about Arlene's story and her plans for more "I'm IN" workshops, join us over at spark.repossible.com.

PART IV

WHEN

"It was like there was a pile of kindling that was in the back of my imagination just waiting there. Once I lit it, it just flared up and I kept getting ideas and ideas."

— Kevin J. Anderson

17

INTRODUCTION: KINDLING

"The best time to plant a tree was 20 years ago. The second best time is now."

— CHINESE PROVERB

My dad passed away in 2015. I struggle sometimes to understand the idea in time that he'll never come back. The idea of never being the word I can't really comprehend.

In 2014, my boys were 8 and 10 when we "did that book project" as they like to refer to it. Never again will Lu (admittedly and voluntarily) write a little story about farting and aliens.

There is no way I could now get my 15-year-old-hair-in-his-armpits son Li to sit down a record a chapter of a book he wrote and follow through with it until it was right.

But frankly, I got what I wanted. What I have today is the audio of each boy reading their own chapters. It's priceless. Of all of the Side Effects and Benefits of this entire operation, those two audio files are what I cherish most.

They'll never be 8 and 10 again. In fact, it was only during that year.

This section is called When. For me, the answer to that question is simple: now.

Or to put it even more strongly: It's now or never.

I smell a chapter title...

IT'S NOW OR NEVER
PLEASE DON'T WAIT 12 YEARS

"Every now and then a man's mind is stretched by a new idea or sensation, and never shrinks back to its former dimensions."

— Oliver Wendell Holmes, Jr.

12 years from now will be too late.

Seth Godin has a habit of writing a few sentences that hit home. Did I mention he writes Every Single Day? What a concept. Here's Seth:

"Twelve years from now, your future self is going to thank you for something you did today, for an asset you began to build, a habit you formed, a seed you planted. Even if you're not sure of where it will lead, today's the day to begin."

— Seth Godin

I waited 10 years. Here's a quick timeline of my early author career:

1. 2004: wrote a book,
2. 2014: wrote next book.

What happened in between? Easy: nothing--at least not as far as my dream of writing books. Did you do the math there? 2014 - 2004 = 10. Those are years. I can't get those back.

What's most interesting about Seth's post is this part:

your *future self* is going to thank (the *present*) *you*

We're not talking about:

- The press,
- The Oscars,
- Your kids,
- Your spouse,
- Your fans,
- Your worldwide tour promoter.

We're talking about:

1. Your future self
2. thanking you (that is, your present self).

It's so simple. So powerful. So hard.
Yet so easy.
It begins with the first step.
What are you waiting for?
Please don't wait 12 years. Your future self will thank your current self.

∽

Flashback
Red chair. Living room. San Francisco. March 3, 2014.
Sitting with my 8-year-old son after having read a so-so

children's book, my past, present, and future passed before my eyes. I (past) had wanted to be a writer, I (present) wasn't a writer and I (future) wanted to be a writer. For some reason, it hit me that this was one of those now-or-never moments.

19

RICH

ARE CHINASAURS EXTINCT?

"The future is wide open. I may actually go back and get that law degree someday."

— GRETCHEN CARLSON

As much as I don't like the "threat" of It's Now or Never, it really comes down to...It's Now or Never.

My 15-year-old-almost-shaving son would need a large pizza, a new PS4 game, and an unlimited mobile data plan to even get near a microphone to record the audiobook version of the book we wrote.

When my kids were 8 and 10, it was Then or Never. Technically speaking, 4 years later is equivalent to never.

My partner in crime for the Markree Castle series, Rich Robinson, was busy with a project called "Chinasaurs" around the time we were working on Markree Castle.

He lives in Beijing, China, (thus the book name) and had worked together with a paleontologist and his two boys to put together a book about dinosaurs in China.

They sketched out storyboards, met with the paleontologist, and had most of an outline. They were going strong and then, somewhere along the way, from an unknown corner of the universe, timed just right to collide with their enthusiasm, youth, and efforts, life happened.

The project never got finished.

As Rich and I spoke about it, it was clear that it would most probably never get done. His boys are now older and about as interested in dinosaurs as my boys are interested in castles in Ireland.

In case that wasn't clear, think about a thing you sort of have to do but don't really truly have to do, others would like you to do it, they'd even like you to be interested in it but you're clearly not, and the only reason you might think of doing the thing is to please them, but if you're a 15-year-old-boy, that's not really in your wheelhouse.

The boys weren't too beat up about it, but Rich was.

It's also difficult to measure if the boys might have thought too much differently had they finished the project.

For pictures of Rich's boys' storyboards and the Chinasaurs project, visit spark.repossible.com.

∼

Flashback
Bathroom Mirror, Driebergen, The Netherlands
"I think I need to shave. Dad, can we buy some razors?"
Just recently turned 15-year-old Li doesn't not remember
   Kite Hill, but mostly because it's how we walked home
   from school for six years. But "The Secret of Kite Hill"?
   Oh yeah, that book project we did together.

20

LIZZ
WAITING FOR THE PERFECT TIME

"If you look to your past or even your present to see why you are here or what your purpose is, you may get stuck in a limited view of yourself. Instead, look beyond your years here on earth, reconnect with the divine, and bring forth your soul's legacy into the present moment."

— DEBBIE FORD

Lizz would love to write a book together with her kids. She'd love to write a book at all. I'm pretty sure she'd be rather pleased with writing anything. There are few things holding her back:

1. Reality
2. Time
3. Pressure
4. The present moment
5. Decisions
6. Excuses
7. Other stuff

We could probably narrow that down to just two:

1. Reality
2. Other stuff

"Why is Lizz a chapter of this book if she hasn't yet completed the experiment?" I hear you whispering to yourself.

She's in here exactly because she hasn't yet completed the experiment. She's here so we can root her on. So I can call her out and, yep, put her in the spotlight, and remind her (and me and us and you) that:

We're rooting for you.

My intention with this book is not to show you how fantastic we all are who created these magnificent experiments with their kids and they're now leading global initiatives.

My intention is to create.

My intention is to start with nothing and create something, together with a younger person we love. Oh, and finish it.

Lizz, you're here to lead us. We're following in your footsteps. We're rooting for you. We're behind you all the way. We want to see what you come up with.

This is an experiment. We cannot fail. There is no failure. There is only learning, experiencing, getting done, and moving on to the next adventure.

That's why Lizz gets her own chapter.

21

LORENA
WE CAN ALWAYS FINISH IT TOMORROW

"Never put off till tomorrow what you can do the day after tomorrow."

— Mark Twain

Lorena and her son created a fantastic adventure complete with colorful characters, funny names, and a moving story of how to fit in with others when you're different.

They worked on the story together, built out the characters with even more detail, and even gave the book a title: "Kungi Kanga."

When I asked her where the story was today, the pain and regret were evident in her voice.

The story was in a file on her computer. As we talked about it more, she even went so far as to say that the characters were imprisoned within the plastic walls of her computer and have never been out to see the light of day or transformed into ink on a page of a book.

Lorena is an author who has written several books, but the one that possibly pains her the most is the one that is trapped in the prison of the past.

Although there is not yet a happy ending to this story, there could be (especially with encouragement from us, the readers of this book and participants in this adventure). The file is still on her computer. She hasn't deleted it.

In fact, the prison where this story still lives is the worst kind of prison. This kind of prison has no locks and no doors yet it's difficult to escape.

The key to setting the story free lies not in the past and not in the future but in the present. The key to bringing her son's imagination to life lies in the simple but not always easy task of taking action to finish a project started long ago.

Often the longer we wait, the more difficult it is to reinvigorate something from the past but it's still possible. Easier, as I'm sure you can imagine at this point, is to finish what we begin without delay, without unnecessary doubt, and can take a line from a child's innocent and pure playbook and ask not why the story should come to life but why not?

In this book, I almost don't dare tell you that rekindling an old project is even harder than beginning a new project because I don't want you to to be discouraged and never begin. For the most part, I believe that starting the project releases enthusiasm, confidence, and an accountability from yourself and your team to keep going.

Perhaps it's not necessarily that finishing a project is more difficult than starting a project but in terms of pain, guilt, and regret, not finishing a project is far worse than not starting.

∼

Flashback
Hallway, Driebergen, The Netherlands
There was some old paint on a door frame. It had been
   there "forever." But of course it hadn't been there
   forever. It was maybe 6 months. Maybe it was a year.
   Maybe it actually was forever.
But I walked by it everyday and saw it. I noticed it. I knew

I would "someday" get a knife or one of those spatula scraper things and clean it off.
But I never did.
Until I did.
What had bugged me on a daily basis for what seemed like eternity took approximately 8 minutes to solve.
Let's do a little math, shall we?
5 seconds of annoyance x 184 days = just way too much
8 minutes to solve or wait another 5 seconds for X number of days?
Could it be that simple to fix the one-time job for a lifetime of no longer daily annoyances?
Could it be that simple?

PART V

HOW

"A person who never made a mistake never tried anything new."

— Albert Einstein

INTRODUCTION: SPARKS

"Education is not the filling of a pail, but the lighting of a fire."

— William Butler Yeats

This is the section where I explain how to do it.

I have talked with lots (no, really, way too many) of people about Spark. Often when I get into the How of it all, they'll say:

"But it's easy for you to say, you've already done it."

Let's do some more examples, just for kicks:

- The marathon runner runs marathons. (Because he's already in shape.)
- The brain surgeon does brain surgery. (He studied it and, hopefully, has had lots of experience performing brain surgeries.)
- I have written 5 books with my kids. (Because I got that first one started and done.)

Did I just put myself in a bullet list with marathon runners and brain surgeons? Absolutely.

They all had a Day One. That day when they knew nothing, couldn't do anything, were beginners.

After my MBA, I was a Management Consultant. The big secret behind management consulting is that you just need to be one step ahead (or off to the side) of the client.

We only need to be one step ahead of our kids.

"Wait. Dad. Sorry, but what did you say we were going to do in February? Did you say we're going to write a book together?"

Cue answer card: "Yes!"

See, you're already ahead of them.

Now that you're brimming with confidence, let's jump right into car repair.

23

REPLACE CAR ENGINE IN TWO STEPS
HERE'S EXACTLY HOW TO DO IT

> "Everything from airplanes to kitchen blenders and even chopsticks comes with an instruction manual. Children, despite all their complexity, do not."
>
> — Lawrence Kutner

I was a huge fan of the "Car Talk" radio show. Two brothers who were car mechanics talked about car repair. I'm not a car guy. You'd think, "Bradley, why in the world would you listen to a radio show about car repair?"

It was basically a comedy hour. The two guys were so funny it didn't matter what they were talking about.

One of my favorite pieces was when they explained how to replace a car engine. It was a perfect example of Simple But Not Easy. I'll let you in on their secret instruction manual.

How to replace a car engine:

1. Remove old engine.
2. Drop in new engine.

There you have it. It's not wrong. But it also doesn't really give you many details.

Here you go. Now that we're deep into this book, I'm just going to go ahead and give you the:

Instruction Manual to write a book with your kids

1. Find kid.
2. Write a book together.

There you have it. We're done! Simple. But not necessarily easy.

We also don't need to go to the gym. Seriously, what do you call those conveyor belts to run on? What, is the pavement outside broken? Put on shoes. Go outside. Move legs. Return home at some point.

Kids don't read instruction manuals to learn how to ride a bike. They hop on, crash, and do better the next time. Soon, they get it.

It's that simple.

No, really. It is.

I can (and will be happy to) give you all kinds of instructions and tips and tricks, tactics and strategies, and dive deep into the case studies of my own kids and those who have granted access to the stories of their own adventures in this book, but it's going to come down to you and a kid and writing a book (or painting a canvas or composing a song or whatever).

Just in case you're searching in this book for How To Do It, I'll put it down here again:

1. Find kid.
2. Write a book together.

Here, this will help: a deadline.

Let's move on to the next chapter.

24

HALFWAY WILL NEVER FINISH
IT WILL BE DONE BY THE END OF THE MONTH

"The best thing for my creative process is a deadline."

— Jeff MacNelly

I specifically remember a math word problem in school in which one of the race contestants would get halfway to the finish line with each effort. At the beginning, he was way out in front. With one step, he'd gone halfway to the finish line.

The trick, the joke, the bad news comes when you realize that halfway will never get to the finish line. Sure, at the end, the distance will be microscopic, but by definition, he'll never make it.

It doesn't matter how fast you're out of the starting gate or even how quick your pace is.

We want to finish this thing.

The only thing that works for me is a deadline. We have one: the last day of the month.

There, problem solved.

25

CREATE A CONFLICT
YOUR CHILD WILL FIND A WAY TO SOLVE IT

"Every problem has in it the seeds of its own solution. If you don't have any problems, you don't get any seeds."

— NORMAN VINCENT PEALE

I know, I know. I can hear you.
"Hey, that's really cute about the car engine and everything, but I honest and truly don't know where to start."
I get it.
Keep in mind this doesn't need to be a book. But for the sake of simplicity and because I'm the one with the keyboard (at least in this chapter), I'm going to give you the inside scoop on how to write a book with your kids.

Houston, we need a problem.

Kids are remarkably imaginative. Take that glowing device out of their hands for a few minutes and brain cells rejoice and start forming new synapses and connections and are partying like it's 1999.

But they need a challenge. A question. Somewhere to start.

What can you take from your everyday life to stir up a little pandemonium? What can you (at least for the sake of literary beginnings) take away from your child they'll miss dearly? Start with that.

I tend to think in book titles. Here are a few that would rattle my sons:

1. The Perilous Adventure of How Lu Beat Li in 1-on-1 Basketball
2. Is that Dog Barf on my Waffle?
3. Why Lu is So Much Better than Li (Book 1 of the 274-book series written solely by Lu)
4. How My Job at Foot Locker Rocketed My Entrepreneurial Success (clearly non-fiction)
5. The Thanksgiving when I Pulled the Wart off of Aunt Hildegard's Nose
6. New Year's Eve Fireworks Laws (and how to avoid them)

Are these triggering anything? Firing up some really bad story about your cousin and his visit over the holidays?

Here are a few other tried and true tactics:

1. What if you wrote a book that no one would ever see? (except maybe mom)
2. Shoot for the worst book of fiction known to the history of literature--and the shortest.
3. The secret book that only you and your kid knew about.
4. Write a 4-page book with no verbs.
5. Let your child tell a story where your only question is, "Then what happened?" (Keep at it until he falls over or needs food.)

Maybe a non-fiction book would delight your little know-it-all. What are they good at? How could they help someone else with their knowledge? What "How To" book might they write?

Or they might want to jump into research because they want their book to be better and they realize at some point that no, they don't actually know everything and that others know some other things and if they talk to them they might learn something--and can put it in their book and their book will be better, more interesting, and might even develop into a different book.

Gee, where could I have ever heard of this concept?

Or maybe it's fiction and storytelling for your child. I don't know about you, but if I started off with "The Thanksgiving when I Pulled the Wart off of Aunt Hildegard's Nose" to a kid and let them tell me the story, I think I'd be in for a rollicking ride of imagination.

For more ideas, questions, and starting blocks, come on over and join Camp Spark at spark.repossible.com.

26

MEG
ELEMENTAL P

"The future belongs to those who believe in the beauty of their dreams."

— Eleanor Roosevelt

If you grew up in the United States (and maybe other English-speaking countries, let me know if you recognize this...), you learn the alphabet by a song made up of all 26 letters. Well, a "song" might be a big word. It's just a sing-song melody of the letters but as soon as anyone who recognizes the tune they'll jump in and finish.

When Meg was 5 years old, she thought the part where they spell out "L M N O P" was actually "Elemental P."

Here's Meg with the play by play of how it went down.

"It's all stick figures. I did the broad strokes on the figures but he did all of the outfits on them. He's very much into clothes and designing. They all have pretty elaborate outfits on them.

We give the books away at schools and the kids are mesmerized by Matthew. Authors are a big deal. Every time they read a book, they learn about authors, they know about authors, they read authors in a series. Matthew is in 3rd grade now. They're blown away.

He was in kindergarten when we wrote it. He was in 1st grade when we finally got it published.

He's creative. I'm not particularly creative. I'm a lawyer.

Of course he wants to write another one.

He loved books. I read probably 4 books to him per night from the time he was 6 months old.

It's good. Kids like it. They really respond to it. It's all educational. He insists on personally handing out every book to every kid.

The first one he was nervous and now he's all in."

On the back cover of the book, Meg thanks her mother (Matthew's grandmother) "for believing in our dream and helping to make it come true."

It turns out, this adventure, this experiment is not always just about the two of you. It might extend beyond your household and touch and involve and even need the support of those around you.

A father of one of Matthew's classmates helped out with printing. Another friend connected with an author for advice.

It didn't start our simple and easy. But it became both. Together with people who came to them to help, who were inspired by what they were doing, they made it happen.

It became bigger than just the two of them. It became bigger than 1 + 1. It was their experiment together.

27

WANT TO TRULY LEARN SOMETHING? LEARN IT THROUGH YOUR KIDS.
I WAS PRETTY SURE I KNEW EVERYTHING. TURNS OUT I KNEW NOTHING.

"If you're not making mistakes, then you're not doing anything. I'm positive that a doer makes mistakes."

— John Wooden

You think you know about a topic? See what your kids learn during a (school) project then compare that with what you thought you knew.

Learn through what your kids learn.

Don't read the article or the book yourself and come to your own conclusions.

1. Read the article (or sections of a book) **aloud** to your kids and then do not give them your opinion.
2. **Listen** to their first comments.
3. **Ask** further questions. (Still not giving your opinion.)
4. Allow the awkward **silence.** Listen to what they have to say about it when you don't talk about it.

You're learning about the topic, but you're also learning how your child is learning.

1. What did they pick up from what you read?
2. Was it anything close to what you got out of it?
3. Did they pick up important details?
4. Did they miss something important?
5. Were they listening at all?

This is a good way to see how much comprehension they actually have from content.

John Wooden

Famed UCLA Basketball coach John Wooden didn't like being called "The Wizard of Westwood" as he mentions below (see quotes) because a wizard was seen as "being some sort of magician" and to the contrary, he believed deeply in hard work, making mistakes, and sweating the details.

He didn't like being call a wizard, but we could at least call him a wise philosopher.

I consciously added this chapter to the book partly because it was a learning experience through doing a project together with my son but also because John Wooden has been a hero of mine since I was a kid and I'm proud to feature him anywhere I possibly can.

Share the quotes below with your child and see if any of them resonate.

John Wooden Quotes

1. If you're not making mistakes, then you're not doing anything. I'm positive that a doer makes mistakes.
2. I'm no wizard, and I don't like being thought of in that light at all. I think of a wizard as being some sort of

magician or something, doing something on the sly or something, and I don't want to be thought of in that way.

3. Whatever you do in life, surround yourself with smart people who'll argue with you.
4. It's the little details that are vital. Little things make big things happen.
5. Be true to yourself, help others, make each day your masterpiece, make friendship a fine art, drink deeply from good books – especially the Bible, build a shelter against a rainy day, give thanks for your blessings and pray for guidance every day.
6. Things turn out best for the people who make the best of the way things turn out.
7. I think the teaching profession contributes more to the future of our society than any other single profession.
8. Be more concerned with your character than your reputation, because your character is what you really are, while your reputation is merely what others think you are.
9. The most important thing in the world is family and love.
10. Do not let what you cannot do interfere with what you can do.
11. It isn't what you do, but how you do it.
12. Today is the only day. Yesterday is gone.
13. Don't give up on your dreams, or your dreams will give up on you.
14. The main ingredient of stardom is the rest of the team.
15. Well, your greatest joy definitely comes from doing something for another, especially when it was done with no thought of something in return.
16. You can't live a perfect day without doing something for someone who will never be able to repay you.
17. If I am through learning, I am through.
18. Failure is never fatal. But failure to change can and might be.

Flashback
Kitchen table. Learn from the student.
Then 9-year old Lu did a school project on John Wooden. I thought I knew Coach Wooden pretty well. I even have a signed copy of "Practical Modern Basketball" I got signed by Coach Wooden in person while at a UCLA game maybe around the time I was…9-years old. Of course, I never actually read the book. Turns out I had a lot to learn. About John Wooden. And about learning. I learned more in the short time with Lu and his school project than I had in a lifetime of following the great coach—and not actually reading what he wrote.

Bonus Exercise

I must add this in here as it worked wonders, is oddly easy, and is fun at the same time.

Can't get your kids to do their homework? Turn on the time-lapse video option and let your kid know he's the star and everything he does is being recorded.

Keep it on until they finish their homework. Let them watch it when they're done. I'll make sure I have the video of my son working on his John Wooden report at spark.repossible.com.

Come check it out and if you do one, share yours with us too.

28

HOW TO MAKE FRIENDS AND INFLUENCE...YOUR KIDS
LET'S BRING IN SOME TRIED-AND-TRUE MANAGEMENT TECHNIQUES

> "Don't worry that children never listen to you; worry that they are always watching you."
>
> — ROBERT FULGHUM

When you're working with kids (or, for that matter, adults who act like kids), there are some project management techniques that can be extremely helpful, time saving, and fun.

Fun?

I needed the boys to answer a few questions about their characters in the Kite Hill book. Fun stuff: character traits, magical powers, and "catch phrase."

> *Author's note: this was written when we were working on The Markree Castle series. I'm going to leave it in the present tense from then as it gives the authentic feel of what I was doing at the time.*
>
> *Doctor's note: I think the boys are a little obsessed with In-*

> N-Out Burger. You might want to look into talking with a nutritionist.

1.) Don't edit

As expected, my older son jumped right in. "I know, I know," he said, almost shaking as he couldn't wait to get it out. "I'd have a magic straw that was white and red and when I waved it, I could have any In-N-Out order I wanted!" He waved his invisible wand, "A Double Double!" Waved again, "A vanilla shake!" I think he was hungry...I did pick them up a little late.

Later I learned that he meant that the straw/wand created an actual In-N-Out building! Glad I didn't understand at the time as I liked the visual of the cheeseburger and shake appearing in the forest of Ireland quite magically culinary.

2.) Be enthusiastic about their answers

I didn't have to fake it: I laughed hard and out loud at the In-N-Out magical power. You always think they'll go for flying or invisible cloaks or potions. But the whole vision of In-N-Out was priceless. Enthusiasm? Check!

3.) Listen

Comment on their answers that show you're listening.

"I bet your buddies Dec & Den are going to LOVE your In-N-Out wand!" I said without hesitation or exaggeration.

Dec & Den are their friends who are going to be sharing the pages of adventure in their upcoming book based on a weekend of adventures in a castle in Ireland. "So," I asked in all seriousness ... wow, maybe I was hungry too ... "Can your wand make In-N-Out appear for everyone or just you?"

"For anyone," he said. Oh goodie.

4.) Keep the momentum

If there are less fun questions, sneak those in while the iron is hot. I wanted to gather some "character traits" (e.g. shy, silly, honest, etc.), but wasn't sure how to ask. So I just asked. I got the answers (older boy said, "Honest, good at American football.") and moved on.

5.) Listen

No, it's not a typo. If you can listen (and then listen some more), you've already leaped out of the starting gates.

29

BRAD

WHAT DO YOU THINK ABOUT YOUR DAD?

"I was not naturally talented. I didn't sing, dance or act, though working around that minor detail made me inventive."

— STEVE MARTIN

Brad was just asking for trouble.
    Oh, I know, here's a way to challenge the universe as we know it:

1. Set up a camera,
2. Turn it on,
3. Sit with your daughter (or any available child),
4. Ask them questions. Like an interview.
5. You could ask "safe" questions like, "What does Christmas mean to you?" or "In general, do you think teenagers are dumb?"
6. Or you could invite immediate danger and ask them things like, "What do you think of your dad?"
7. Let them speak,
8. Hear them out,

9. Be patient,
10. Listen,
11. Post it on YouTube.

I was good with it all up to #11. He's asking for it.

But this is exactly what he did.

He turned his sons and daughters into actors, performers, and interviewees. Just like that. With a camera. Turned on.

He transformed what might have been "an interesting conversation" that in all probability never would have been remembered by either party involved, into a time capsule of a moment of dad at that time and daughter at that time.

He has different videos of his kids at different times with different topics. I think it would be a neat project to do every year and see how the kids (and the adults) progressed (or digressed...). But I'm getting ahead of myself.

Here you go, here's an easy one (full of potential downside and upside). Just make one video together with your kids.

1. Hit record on your phone,
2. Ask them one question,
3. Listen.

You don't have to post it on YouTube.

Need some questions? I bet Brad has some for us. See his nail-biting cliffhangers over at spark.repossible.com and we'll rustle up some safe questions to ask your kids in an "interview."

Then we'll get to some you only have to ask if you're a daredevil, risk taker, and rockstar. Like Brad.

30

DON'T TALK ABOUT THE PROJECT. START THE PROJECT.
JUMP RIGHT IN.

"In Missouri, where I come from, we don't talk about what we do—we just do it. If we talk about it, it's seen as bragging."

— Brad Pitt

There are a few schools of thought on this topic. Let's try to get them squared away so you know what works best for you.

I'm talking about two different things here:

1. Telling your kids about what you're doing,
2. Telling friends, family, coworkers, and strangers about what you're doing.

We'll make sure to cover both. My main philosophy here is: whatever works.

1.) Tell no one

Kids

The Ideal World. Depending the ages of the kids, this could go both ways. We all hope the kids will be enthusiastic about joining the family endeavor so tell them, have them involved from the start.

Reality Teen Drama. If I so much as mention "work" or "project" to any male young person above the age of, say, 12, they might win the Olympic relay and run away with...the TV remote. I often resorted to underhanded, sleight-of-hand trickery to get to the next stage of our undertaking.

Adults

Have you ever opened up to a friend about something and regretted it the minute they had their first reaction? If you'd like to keep things safe for a while, don't tell anyone what you're doing. If the entire enterprise turns into the biggest disaster in the history of your family, no harm done--and even your family will laugh about it later. Well, maybe much later.

2.) Tell a select few

Kids

Make it a select, exclusive, members-only crew of highly sought out individuals. OK, so even if it's not that, you can easily make it sound like that.

Adults

With the right group, you'll get enthusiastic folks cheering you on and those who don't know won't be bothered by it. If you do this right, you might even pique the interest of those you thought would never be interested. Win win.

3.) Tell everyone

Kids

Go overboard. Tell your kids. Tell their friends. Be overly, annoyingly enthusiastic to the point where your kids will forcibly hold you back from talking about "The Thing We're Doing." This can be lots of fun and get more and more people involved.

Adults

If you're the type who announces, "I'm going to lose 2 pounds by January 31!" and then you actually do it, you might be better off telling everyone this is what you're doing.

∾

Flashback

Corbett Street, San Francisco, Mistake #1

I made the first mistake about talking about "The Book Project" while walking home from school. I quickly changed the subject to something completely different when I got not-exactly-jumping-for-joy responses and remembered this rule: don't talk about what you're going to do, just get started and let them be a part of it. If you're savvy, you'll get them to even want to help. Sound impossible? Very Tom Sawyer and white picket fences, I know.

31

KEEP IT LEGAL, BUT KEEP IT REAL

IT'S SORT OF LIKE COOPERATION, BUT IT'S OCCASIONALLY COMPETITION.

"My parents are very competitive, so we are very competitive as kids. But it's a good kind of competition; it's not a jealousy. You always want to do your best, and if it can't be you, you want it to be your brother or your sister, you know what I mean?"

— Janet Jackson

There might possibly be times, now and again, few and far between, roughly on the schedule of the lunar eclipse, or maybe a meteor shower, where you might need to bring in the big guns, the hired hands, the friends at the table.

Let's take a trip back to the pasta restaurant off Highway 80.

> *Flashback*
> *Spaghetti Factory. Rancho Cordova, California.*
> *I wasn't getting any answers. I wasn't even getting*
> > *responses. I'm not sure there was a pulse. It was time to*
> > *call in the big boys. Or at least, the other boys.*
> *I looked over at Li and Lu's friends sitting at our same table.*
> *"So Aiden, say there's a good guy working at a castle and*

> then there's a bad guy also working at a castle. How are they related?"
> Zero bites of spaghetti and 10 minutes later, I had the next chapter (and an underlying fight for power over the castle) from Li's friend.
> Aiden went back to his spaghetti, I furiously took notes on a napkin, and my boys woke up and wanted in on the action.
> My kids weren't providing the goods. It was clearly time to outsource.

Let's have a quick look at what transpired among the gluten-free pasta with Mizithra cheese and brown butter.

We had a deadline. I was a bit stuck. I needed a fresh perspective on the conflict between the good guy and the bad guy in the Markree Castle series. I asked my team. They were sick of me and much more interested in the bottomless iced tea.

Sure, I could build this up and use big words like:

- Coercion
- Jealousy
- Envy
- FOMO

But let's keep it friendly among friends (and meatballs). Here's the real shining gem in the rough: Aiden was into it. I couldn't even keep up with his imagination and storyline that he just kept building and growing. He was getting more and more into it.

He was having a blast.

See what happened there?

Here I am working on my own kids and *trying* to get them to participate when the boy across the table is *willing* and *able*.

Let's do a quick round up of the table scorecard:

- Able? 4

- Able but not willing? 3
- Not able and not willing? 0
- Able and willing? 1

Work with what you have on hand

My older son is quickly envious of my younger son, so I figured if I could get the younger one involved, the older one would want to be a part of it. I needed the answer from Li, but he wasn't talking.

I asked my younger son the question, "If you could have any magical power, what would it be?"

It's a fun question to be sure, and my younger son went straight into creative imagination mode.

"I could create 'Mini Me' creatures whenever I wanted to. Each little version of me would have a gatling gun and..."

OK, he qualifies for being 100% boy as most creative explorations involve guns, explosions, farts or butts. Better yet if they include all them.

Now that Lu answered and Li was probably simmering with all kinds of imaginative ideas, Li finally answered.

The direct question didn't work. However, the indirect "jealousy" trick worked wonders.

Keep it legal, but keep it real.

32

LINDA
WHAT DO YOU, THE PARENT, LOVE TO DO?

"Writing, film, sculpture, music: it's all make-believe, really."

— Kate Bush

Linda is a musician. She said:

"Music has always been a huge part of my life."

Both she and her husband are in bands. Their children, when they were born, were not born musicians. The parents brought to the children what was close to them, what they were good at, what they loved.

For her father's 80th birthday, they created a parody of a song and performed it. Here's Linda in her own words and my bumbling.

> Me: "You created something. You made this song, you wrote it together in the car on the way there. You performed it with your family for your dad."
>
> Linda: "Yeah."

Me: "Wow."

Me: "You could have all chipped in and got him a chainsaw for his birthday. Some item. Some thing at the store. You created something from nothing. You created a song, there was no song. You did this thing and you gave it to him."

Linda: "It was somewhat conscious. It was something we always thought was so fun. It was always so well received. It was a very satisfying creative process."

Me: "Mom and dad do these parodies, it looks like fun. That's really neat that you do that. But what you did was you brought the kids in and said, 'Hey, not only do mom and dad do this but we're going to bring the kids in and do this together.' You involved them."

Sure, maybe if you're a hired assassin or an astronaut, it might be a little harder to share What You Do and Love with your kids.

But if you're stuck at the point of, "Gee, I'm not creative." or "I don't know what we'd do together." then maybe letting them into a part of your world is an idea.

Not that they have to study the 7-volume "Corporate Tax Law in New York State (updated 2014)" with you, but how could you give them a tiny little glimpse into something you love?

PART VI

CAMPFIRE STORIES

"Life is an adventure, it's not a package tour."

— Eckhart Tolle

33

INTRODUCTION: MATCHES

"We've had bad luck with our kids—they've all grown up."

— CHRISTOPHER MORLEY

I suppose if I'm going to keep going with the whole fire and spark and camping metaphor, I need to keep it going even all the way down here in Part 6.

I've been working on this book for the past four years.

Ever since we wrote some of the first lines of "The Secret of Kite Hill" and I mentioned to anyone (parents or not) what I was doing, there was a reaction. A strong reaction. An emotional reaction. Let's see if I can bring some of them back:

- **Insanity:** "I'm sorry, did you say you're doing this willingly or is this part of your parole violation agreement?"
- **Love:** "That's the most beautiful thing I've ever heard. Your kids are going to thank you someday for this from the bottom of their hearts." (Author's note: I'm not holding my breath, but I think it might arrive before the year 2034.)

- **Guilt:** "Wow, I'm not sure I know my middle daughter's middle name."
- **Cooperation:** "Dude, tell me when you're ready for the next one, I'd love to be a part of it."

Part of the reason I enjoy writing books is because it's an adventure, an experiment, and it helps define who I am for that period in my life.

I don't just write books. I live them.

I talk to random strangers and ask them about a topic in my book. I bore friends to death at dinner parties about whatever hare-brained scheme I have up my sleeve. It becomes a part of me.

This is what I want for you, too.

People like to hear what others are doing when it's a kooky project. I especially love the reaction, complete with a head shake and maybe even one eye partly closed, "I'm sorry, what did you say you were working on?"

Go ahead, try it.

Tell people you're doing one of these things:

1. I have a new project at work. Want to see the PowerPoint?
2. My day today was just like my day yesterday. Should I elaborate?
3. Hey there! I wanted to tell you about that same thing I told you about last time but in more detail. Do you have a spare four hours?

Or you could try this:

1. My daughter and I are doing an experiment to write the worst children's book in the state of Wisconsin. It's about gopher poop worms. Want to see the cover?
2. My son said dogs can talk and he's writing a book about it. It's 13 pages and it's called, "No, I Don't Have to Pee."
3. My 9-year-old daughter is doing research on 9-year-old

girls who can tell stories with their eyes closed. Is Megan here today?

Maybe they'll ask you to step away from the cookie jar. Maybe they'll reconsider the ski weekend plans they had and forget to call you.

But maybe you'll strike a nerve. Maybe you'll make a connection. Maybe you'll make a scene and they'll want to be a part of it.

Maybe nothing will come of it.

Maybe something will come of it.

How are we going to know if we don't experiment?

In the next chapters, I've placed articles that I published over the past four years that have helped me build Spark to what it is today. Maybe they'll be a match to your Spark and ignite some creativity in you and your kids and get this party started.

34

HOW TO INSTILL CREATIVITY IN YOUR CHILDREN IN THREE NOT-SO-EASY STEPS.

YOU'D LIKE YOUR CHILD TO THINK, TO EXPLORE, TO IMAGINE AND CREATE. IT MIGHT TAKE A BIT OF HEAVY LIFTING.

> "It's really difficult working with kids and with babies because they are not cooperative subjects: they are not socialized into the idea that they should cheerfully and cooperatively give you information. They're not like undergraduates, who you can bribe with beer money or course credit."
>
> — PAUL BLOOM

Heavy lifting? Know anyone with a crane?

Lucky for you, I don't give up easily. In fact, I don't give up at all.

- **Goal:** to get my son and his friend to work on a story for the upcoming (illustrated!) next book in the Li & Lu series.
- **Challenge:** he doesn't wanna.

I had asked my son numerous times to "work on his story" with his friend. I knew I needed to ask in a different way (like not use the word "work" or "story" or make a direct request...). I needed to somehow make it more interesting, but I wasn't finding the right connection. He wasn't annoyed with me, he just wasn't excited about it.

I needed a new tactic.

Don't give up. You, hopefully, have more staying power than your kids. You can outlast their stubbornness. Besides, it's for their benefit for you to win this one.

How to recruit your creative team, embrace technology, and squash writer's block.

I needed to find someone who wasn't me. Someone to give the kids just that little head start from which they could continue on. I needed some fresh blood.

I combined several new approaches that I decided to try out.

1. **Friend's mother:** my son and her own son love her. I need her help.
2. **Techno-bribery:** the boys love being on a computer or tablet. I could fall back on my trusty Google Docs and use that as bait to lure them in.
3. **Kill the blank page:** the blank page can be scary and intimidating. Creating from nothing can be stressful. So I started their story for them.

I created a shared Google document and invited my son and his friend to share the document. I also talked to my son's friend's (his name is Toto in the book) mom and ask for her help. She texted me later that afternoon that the shared thing didn't work. It sounded like they weren't going to try to take it any further.

I pushed.

I invited her email address to the shared doc and asked again (read: pleaded) to just try to get them to work on it for 10 minutes. She said she would. I didn't hear anything more about it that day.

The next day, my son said, in passing, in his nonchalant way, "Oh yeah, we worked on it. We finished it."

Wait, what? You did what? You really did? You worked on it together with Toto? You finished?

For the record and for the jury to hear the evidence, I'm just going to highlight those words yet again:

- "We worked on it"
- "We finished it"

(Thank you for your patience, it'll help with the trial later on how they actually did work and finished things.)

They really had worked on it and finished it.

I jumped on my computer and there it was: the shared document with the opening scene of a story was worked on and finished. I read it and was surprised when I laughed out loud at the ending. They did it! They worked together on it and typed and created the end of the story–and it was funny!

The not-so-secret motive behind writing a book with your kids.

I'm not terribly interested in writing the great American novel. I'm not fascinated by the best-seller list. Sure, those are great and I'd love to achieve that (and, actually, I will), but my goals are parallel to those:

- I want to give my kids the gift of creativity.
- I want them to be able to create something from nothing.
- I want them to start and finish a project and own it.
- I want them to be proud of what they did.
- I want them to feel confident in their next project.
- I want them to want their next project to be better than their first and if it isn't, to work on a third project.
- I want to get the ball rolling.
- I want to be the spark.

I succeeded. They succeeded. We succeeded.

35

LOSS LEADERS, SALES, FLEA MARKETS AND 12-YEAR OLDS WHO WANT NEW SHOES.

YOU CAN CALL IT MATH OR YOU CAN CALL IT CURRENCY TO BUY FROZEN SLUSHIES. UP TO YOU.

> "'Priced to sell' - just the phrase makes me smile. When a dealer says all the items in his booth are priced to sell, he means he's tagged them as aggressively as he can to get you to buy them. Don't worry, though, I still haggle. You have to. That's the point of a flea market."
>
> — Nate Berkus

You can hang out with your kids at the park. Or you can hang out with your kids at the park and (secretly) teach them about sales, marketing, and economics.

I can't help it. I'm kind of addicted to teaching my kids at every occasion where I see an opportunity. Which is pretty much all the time. We were at a (sort of) flea market this afternoon. Which, in case you didn't know, is an entire self-contained economic ecosystem.

Requirements: In order for your child to learn, they must want something. Children (well, adults too) usually want something, you just have to figure out what it is. It's usually not that hard: just ask. My 12-year old wants new shoes. He has plenty of shoes, but he wants more shoes. A "luxury" expense so he has to earn his own money for it. He's *motivated*.

Motivation is powerful.

The Economic Environment (AKA the Flea Market)

My boys can't get enough of Donald Duck books. We have hundreds. Well, we had hundreds. We must have sold a hundred today.

But not everyone is a fan of the Donald Duck comic books (yet!). Especially the younger kids probably don't know about them--especially if they can't read. But the Duck books were the bulk of what we were trying to sell today at King's Day (a huge event which celebrates the Dutch king's birthday, although it's really the Queen's birthday, but that's yet another Dutch thing). We needed to get those kids to little kids to our books. Enter the Loss Leader.

> "A loss leader is a pricing strategy where a product is sold at a price below its market cost to stimulate other sales of more profitable goods or services."
>
> — WIKIPEDIA

We just happened to have boxes (and boxes) of plastic garbage (also known as little kid toys). We had hard plastic dinosaurs, Matchbox cars, toy trains and a plethora of worthless trinkets. In other words, a little kid magnet. Their parents can't hold them back, they're drawn to them like a comet to the sun.

We strategically placed our ocean-polluting figurines at the edges of our blanketed shop to suck in the innocent buyers. It worked like magic. We had kids practically brawling over a plastic Godzilla that was missing a wing.

The parents had no choice but to hang around and hover over their child while they sorted through horses, whales and cars. Have you ever closely watched kids looking through toys? It's truly a thing of joy. They are mesmerized. A meteor could strike the neighboring blanket and the jolt to the planet might only make them flinch to the point where they drop the petroleum-based giraffe and pick up the 3-wheeled train car.

Unless mom and dad are being called away to speak at the United Nations, they're sticking around until Junior decides between the purple camel and the naturally-weapon-heavy stegosaurus. They can't say no. In fact, you can help them to not say no by making the kid catnip absolutely...free.

Boom and just like that you understand what a Loss Leader is. Pretty fun stuff, right? This is how I explained it to my 12-year old today in play-by-play action-packed commentary. Wait, it gets better.

BONUS: if you happen to have a 10-year old around, put them to work as a "greeter." Let them charm mom and dad by talking about how he played with the pterodactyl and it possibly altered the path of his life's purpose. He should be cute and barely make eye contact with adults and mostly focus on doing tricks with his kendama. Gets 'em every time.

So while Junior is in a heated discussion (with himself) about which animal to take home and cherish until death do they part, mom and dad are checking out what else is on offer. What else is on offer is a huge variety of educational material that could propel Junior to reading at a high-school level after just 27 (low-cost) Donald Ducks. And guess what? We just happen to have at least 27 Donald Ducks available for immediate purchase and delivery. No shipping and handling fees!

With that free Loss Leader securely in Junior's iron-fisted grip, the deal is just about done. A cocktail of guilt, education reform and that-10-year-old-was-so-sweet-to-Junior-we-have-to-buy-a-few-books and mom and dad are picking up their new favorite comic book series. At least two, sometimes four or five, one guy bought a box of Donald Ducks and an entire collection of Dolfje Weerwolfje.

Did you follow what happened here? We gave away a free plastic dinosaur and made a multiple-unit sale.

Let's summarize the entire transaction. Because there's a lot going on.

1. The **kid** is thrilled with his plastic whatever that he'll probably lose before he gets home. But he has the memory of a goldfish so he's just inherently happy and will have forgotten about the entire day by then anyway and will just wonder when dinner is.
2. We've supplied the **parents** with enough reading material to read to their son in bed for the next three years. Value? Eternal and limitless joy. Score!
3. My **10-year old** helped a little boy choose his gift and built his own confidence as he felt useful to the small boy. He's smiling and proud.
4. My **12-year old** is $14 closer to the new shoes he doesn't need.
5. I got rid of four pounds of books we've read 87 times each and I got to teach my kids about economics.

Let me count: that's win + win + win + win + win.

We're not even to the best part. All of this doesn't even come close to what really happened here.

Today I got to:

1. talk to my boys,
2. hang out with them in the park in the sun and drink overly sugary drinks that they're never allowed to have,
3. teach them what I know without them knowing that I was teaching them anything.

We didn't sit down and use paper or calculators. There wasn't a textbook anywhere. We joked about which kids were going to see the dinosaurs. We were **learning by experience.** We were instilling knowledge into their brains by doing, through real-life situations with real money and real people. We didn't know the outcome of any transaction beforehand so there was the element of adventure and risk.

If I improved their lives just a smidgen, it's a good day.

If they learned something through experience, it's a great day.

It's just a single day, just a day like any other, but I taught my boys something and that's the biggest win.

I am 100% certain my boys would have no idea what I'm going on and on about here, maybe they will when they hit university. But I have the biggest smile on my face as I write this because today was both just another day and yet it was the greatest day. It's possible to make it both.

What are you going to do with a regular Saturday? It's up to you.

36

MAKE MONEY, TEACH YOUR KIDS MATH, AND CLEAN THE HOUSE...AT THE SAME TIME.
WHAT IF VACUUMING WERE A SPORT? WITH PRIZES?

> "In my school, the brightest boys did math and physics, the less bright did physics and chemistry, and the least bright did biology. I wanted to do math and physics, but my father made me do chemistry because he thought there would be no jobs for mathematicians."
>
> — STEPHEN HAWKING

Make money? Teach math? Clean the house? At the same time? (Gather up thick French accent:) Impossible!

In fact, some days, any of those alone seem impossible.

You just need to get creative.

The challenge: we need to clean the house before we leave tomorrow and the kids need to help. It's not going to be fun. Oh yeah, they need to study math. Making money would be fun, but sounds like a long shot.

Here's the Deal

Whenever "work" or "study" or "learning" is even whispered, the kids seem to magically come down with acute cases of deafness, miraculous whole-body paralysis, and calls for emergency bowel movements. They'll say anything. But too bad for them, we need to get out of this house and it needs to be done. We also need to learn some math.

The Goals

Clean the house (no, ALL of us).

Learn math (4th & 6th grade). We're going for functions today such as: sum, percentage, and differences.

Make money in the process (that one is up to me, you'll see).

Forget studying math, let's use math to learn it. Don't even use the word study. It's taboo. What a concept. Let's even throw in how to build and use a spreadsheet, how to look at statistics, and for a bonus: let it do things that are hard to do in our heads (like comparison graphs).

Clean the House

Kids are good with tasks and lists and especially crossing things off lists when we're done. We almost started with a pad of paper this morning, but I decided to go use Google Sheets (Google's version of spreadsheets) to build a spreadsheet and make charts and graphs. More on that below under Making Money.

But I mention it because it helps with motivation. They like to see a list, they like to see it being shortened (or crossed off or checked). I figured out how to make a pie chart with tasks completed and not yet completed so they could see progress.

Imagine this, dear parent friend: together we typed up the list (it's in Dutch in the image but you get the idea) and in order to mark a task from "Nee" to "Ja" (No to Yes on the completed column), my son raced off to pack his suitcase. Let me repeat those words as I don't write them often. I'll even bold them:

"...my son raced off to pack his suitcase."

If you're a parent of young blobs, you'll be happy enough already. But wait, it gets better.

Learn Math

Disclaimer: I was a math major. I like math. I like the yes and no, right or wrong of it. I think it's fun. I apologize to those in advance who thought math was daily torture. It can be fun!

My kids also like math...they just don't really know what it is in real life. They secretly like it as long as we don't call it math. Enter our spreadsheet of hours and tasks. Just a bunch of numbers, right? Boooooorrrrriiiiinnnnnnggggg! How about a chart? How about a chart of the percentage of tasks completed that changes automatically when we mark a task completed?

Trust me, dear non-math-loving parent, kids like progress. Especially seeing it visually.

Word Problems

Wow, I'm truly my father's son. I actually asked my son this today as we were getting started:

"Yes, there are 12 hours of work, but those are "man hours." If we split them up among the 4 of us, how many hours does each of need to work?"

He was thrilled with the answer (it's 3 in case you skipped 5th grade division).

"So we only have to work 3 hours each and we'll be done? Let's get started!"

I need to apologize again as I don't hear this too much in my house when it comes to actual work:

"Let's get started!" quoted 11-year old when he figured out that he didn't need to individually work 12 hours, but only 3.

I probably went a little overboard with my columns "Estimated Time Worked" and "Actual Time Worked" but I wanted them (and me) to have an idea of what we estimated a task would take and how long it actually took. It was pretty difficult to explain that I had to add a half an hour of my time to helping my son put new sheets on the beds because he needed help with the fitted sheets. So he still worked an hour, but I had to add a half an hour to my time (also increasing the total time worked).

Make Money

I'm a big fan of Google Apps. For example, their documents app (Google Docs) and their spreadsheets (Google Sheets). It's what I used to build the spreadsheet and embedded charts and graphs in our work today. Some time ago, Google approached me because I had promoted their Google Apps for your own domain so much and had so many people sign up with them that they supplied me with coupon codes for Google Apps.

If you know and use Gmail, you know that it's free and you also get all of those Google Apps for free. The difference is that your email address is yourname@gmail.com. With Google Apps for your domain, your email address is you@yourdomain.com. I like this because for our personal addresses, I have my whole family on there and we can easily share things like spreadsheets and documents (we also did my 11-year-old's book report on Google Apps tonight) and they're all under our domain name with our unique email addresses. I just think it's more professional (not to mention long term) to have you@yourdomain.com rather than yourdorkynickname2012@gmail.com.

Another disclaimer: yes, I'm going to make money cleaning the house and teaching my kids math. How do you make money? It's just getting creative with how you do things and how you teach others. How could you help them and make a buck at the same time? In the ideal situation, they're thankful you gave them a tool to achieve something and you make a bit of (kinda) passive income.

Google Apps costs $50 per year per user. But you're probably paying that if you pay for email somewhere else. I have coupons that save 20% ("If the full cost is $50 per year, what does it cost if there is a savings of 20%?"…it's down to $40) per user per year for the first year.

If you'd like to sign up for Google Apps so you too can clean your house and teach your kids math, here's your coupon for Google Apps. [update: I think I still have some coupon codes lying around if you really want one, just ask me]

Actual Results

It's now 8 PM and somehow 12 hours divided by 4 didn't equal 3. Maybe we need to revise the spreadsheet. That's OK, my son now knows how to do that. In fact, he's been working on the spreadsheet more than he was working on vacuuming. One last quote just to make me happy and remember this day:

> "… he's been working on the spreadsheet."

In the long run, I'm happier that he's learning how to work a spreadsheet and also what the charts and graphs do and how to read them. It's a trade-off any parent wouldn't mind: learning math for vacuuming?

This is exactly my goal: doing one thing while (secretly?) learning another without reminding them they're learning something. See how that worked?

On that note, I'll go finishing vacuuming the bedroom because even though Einstein and Descartes have sorta finished their "math" for the day, we didn't actually finish cleaning up.

It's the price I pay for being the Spark for my kids.

HOW WOULD YOUR OWN KID SELL HIS OWN BOOK?
ONCE THE BOOK IS DONE, THE REAL CREATIVITY MIGHT TAKE ROOT.

"Logic will get you from A to B. Imagination will take you everywhere."

— ALBERT EINSTEIN

How do your kids find the books they read? How can they apply that to selling their own book?

I asked my boys on our now famous 12-block walk home from school, "So when the book is out, how should we promote it?"

My 9-year old is not usually motivated by money, but was inspired when we sold a bunch of stuff on Craigslist this weekend and since he helped clean things up, he got a cut of the profits.

Working on your "book project" doesn't only mean fleshing out character traits and plot lines. Get them into the promotion of the book and see what they come up with.

I started early in the walk so we'd have time for lots of ideas. The dog ate some poop along the way, so it threw off our concentration, but by the time we got to Kite Hill, we were rolling in ideas (not poop).

I'm going to get this more or less in their words below.

Li's 5 Best Ways to Promote your Book

1. **Tell everyone in your class.** Get your friends to buy it.
2. **Make a book trailer.** A short film about the book. (Li didn't say "book trailer" but he said something like a short film about the book and the characters).
3. **Create a print book version.** Because more people read paper than on a Kindle.
4. **Make a Kindle version.** Because Li has a Kindle and it's easy to buy books on it (Editor's note: a little too easy, in fact).
5. **Pay for ads.** "But it's really expensive," Li added. We talked about how it depends on where it's advertised. Maybe if it's in their school newsletter, not so much, but more if it's the San Francisco Chronicle.

Lu's 5 Top Ways to Promote your Book

1. **Make a movie.** Get it on Netflix. "That way, everyone can see it." We talked about how this might be quite an undertaking …
2. **Make an ad.** Can make a little video and put it on YouTube. Just a thing that says, "It's awesome."
3. **Back cover blurb.** Based on what Lu said, this sounds like a blurb, why the book is so good, a little bit about it.
4. **Funny examples of book on back cover.** Lu showed me the back of his Big Nate books when we got home and they do a very animated job of promotion: examples from the book, promotional blurbs, even little incomplete lists that you can fill out. Fun stuff!
5. **Bribery.** Give some extra money to the people who work at the book store so they put it at the front of the store.

(Editor's note: I am laughing out loud as I write this as I love that he thought of this on his own!)

How would your kids promote what you worked on together? Think they never think about this stuff? Well, maybe they don't, but if you ask them and give them a few blocks of walking (and few other distractions), they might surprise you.

PART VII

GLOW

"Success consists of going from failure to failure without loss of enthusiasm."

— Winston Churchill

PART VII

GLORY

38

SPARK CAMPFIRE
BEYOND THE BOOK

"Every successful individual knows that his or her achievement depends on a community of persons working together."

— Paul Ryan

There is a Spark world beyond these pages. It's called Spark Campfire not only to continue on my whole sparks and kindling and fire analogies, but because I see it as a community coming together and sharing stories.

Here's a bullet list of words that come to mind when I think of what Spark Campfire will become:

1. community
2. stories
3. collections
4. laughing
5. contests for the worst 14-page book of all time
6. marshmallows
7. cooperation
8. co-creating

9. tears of frustration
10. tears of joy
11. audiobook chapters recorded by kids
12. a mom's first novel
13. a dad's dream come true
14. uncles who write books with their nieces
15. stuff I can't even imagine here
16. adventure
17. play

I tend to see things visually. I get these movie scenes in my mind and it's often how I write—I just get down what I see as fast as I can in words.

The visuals keep coming and when I have this, I know I'm usually onto something. I see more of them.

I see kids laughing at their parents (as well as with them).

A mother crying because her daughter was more creative than they ever imagined and telling her story opened up a part of her she hadn't ever witnessed.

An uncle who gets to know his niece better.

A young author who finally has an audience—her parents.

Strangers helping other strangers promote each other's books.

Maybe a grandma helping out her son who's helping out his niece.

A young boy who comes out of his shell and spills his imagination onto the page.

I see lots of things in Spark Campfire. What might you see?

If there are marshmallows, we might even get Li & Lu to visit.

Want to be a part of it? Come see what we're cooking up over at spark.repossible.com.

39

QUESTIONS FOR PARENTS
PRETEND IT'S CAMP AND YOU CAN ASK ANYTHING

"You ask me a question. I have a blank mind. You ask me a question, and the question is informed, and you're interested, and now my mind starts popping. That's what conversation is. That's what communicating is."

— MELISSA LEO

This book is not just a book. Well, sure, what you have in your hands is a book, but that's like saying you have a match in your hand and paper in the other. Stuff is going to happen.

1. I have questions. You have answers.
2. You have questions. I have answers.

What happened with you? Care to share?
Here are some questions I'd love to hear your answers to—as would others who are stuck or recently unstuck.

1. What sparked the initial interest?

2. How did you create and develop your child's interest in this project?
3. What hesitations did you and your kids have to overcome?
4. How did you negotiate, navigate, and partner through the creative process?
5. What were the sticking points that slowed or stalled the process? How did you overcome them?
6. How did everyone view the end product of your collective work?

AFTERWORD

Just after we finished "The Secret of Kite Hill" and I talked about what the boys and I had done I planned to write this book.

It's been 4 years.

I would say "I can't believe I finally did it." except that I can believe it.

Because ever since "Every Single Day," I just get stuff done.

Maybe not fast, maybe not perfect, but I'll get it done.

Spark is now a thing. It's done. It's here.

I'm ready for it to come to life.

I hope you'll share it with me.

ACKNOWLEDGMENTS

This book was the biggest collaborative effort I've ever been a part of.

My mantra for 2018 was Better Together and I can now say with all confidence that things are certainly better together.

I couldn't have done this without the help, stories, and generosity from:

- Rina Mae Acosta
- Arlene Pe Benito
- Maggie Daniels
- Colleen Golafshan
- Linda Hamilton
- Meg Leal
- Adwynna MacKenzie
- Lizz Mendez
- Matt Michel
- John Muldoon
- Gavin Reese
- Rich Robinson
- Brad Silverman
- Lorena Veldhuijzen

- Craig Young

But what's fun about Spark is that this book isn't the end. There is so much more we can play with. I see this list growing with more families and stories and the unknown.

Maybe you'll be next?

RELATIONSHIP

Building a relationship with readers is one of the best things about writing.

I occasionally send an email with details about **new books, sneak peeks** into Works In Progress, early bird **deals**, as well as exclusive, **Readers Only insights** into the writing and publishing process.

For Spark, it all lights up at spark.repossible.com.

ABOUT THE AUTHOR

Bradley Charbonneau is an "unstoppable writing machine."

He can't not write. Writing gives him pleasure, perspective, and the chance to overuse the letter "p" whenever he feels like it.

He doesn't take himself terribly seriously—except for that daily writing habit he's got going on. He's truly reached Part 7: Glow and isn't heading back down ever again.

All he really wants to do is tell stories, travel with his wife to oddball destinations by rickety transport, shoot baskets with his boys, try to perfect the burrito outside of California, and whisper the secrets of freedom and deep joy to whomever is within earshot and shares even the slightest inkling of curiosity.

He currently lives in a little town outside of Utrecht in The Netherlands with his wife Saskia, famous two young boys of "The Adventures of Li & Lu" fame, and their at-least-as-famous dog Pepper.

This is Bradley's fourteenth book.

It is far, far, far from his last.

Find, ask, discuss, play at:
bradleycharbonneau.com

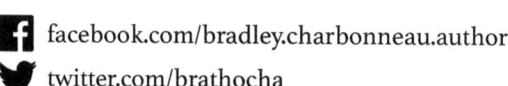

facebook.com/bradley.charbonneau.author
twitter.com/brathocha
instagram.com/brathocha

ALSO BY BRADLEY CHARBONNEAU

Most of my books are also available as audiobooks (which I giddily narrate). Search for my name at your favorite audiobook distributor, slip on your headphones, and let me take you away.

Repossible

Repossible

Every Single Day (+ Playbook)

Ask

Dare

Create

Decide

Meditate

Spark

Surrender

Play

Elevate

Frequency

Every Single Day

Every Single Day Playbook

Every Single Day Kids

Every Single Day Teens (I want to write this one because I want to read this one...)

Every Single Day Parents

Charlie Holiday

Now Is Your Chance (1)

Second Chance (2)

Chance of a Lifetime (3)

For Creatives

Audio for Authors

Meditation for Creatives (2020)

Shorts

Secret Bus to Paradise

Where I (Already) Am

Pass the Sour Cream

A Trip to Hel

Drive-By Dropping

Li & Lu

The Secret of Kite Hill (1)

The Secret of Markree Castle (2)

The Key to Markree Castle (3)

The Gift of Markree Castle (4)

Driehoek (5)

Really Old ...

urban travel guide SAN FRANCISCO

THE END

Thank you for reading "Spark."
 Books don't often have "The End" anymore, so I thought I'd make sure we're really done here.
But of course it's just the beginning.
I hope to see you around the campfire where we can see what lights up, warm up around the fire, and get our glow on.

www.ingramcontent.com/pod-product-compliance
Lightning Source LLC
Chambersburg PA
CBHW071509040426
42444CB00008B/1561